Based *On* A **Love**

Story/*Poems*

Poems by Danielle BlaiQ

Based On A Love Story

ISBN-13: 978-0615814520
ISBN-10: 0615814522

Printed in the United States of America

Permissions
C/O: Danielle B
PO BOX 1104
Durham NC 27702

The names in this book have been changed/abbreviated or legally permitted to be used to protect the individuals involved. All events are described in likeness and not actuality. No part of this book intended to duplicate factual, personal, or private information from affiliates personal or private of the known author.

Based *On* A *Love*

Story/*Poems*

Based *On* A **Love**

Story/*Poems*

Table *of* Contents

Dedicated *to:*

my gorgeous nieces, my handsome nephews & my beautiful unborn child

so **that** your Legacy does

not begin at ground zero

" Oh that my words were now written! Oh that they were printed in a book! "

-Job 19:23

The *Poet's* Note

Thank you for sharing your resources (money, time, energy) reading this book. This isn't a book - this is a poetic rant. *Based On A Love Story* is a collection of heart-rants that over some years I've written. I'd been moving around so much that I became afraid of losing all of my poems. I didn't know where I would end up, so I put my poetry in the one place I could always find it: out in the universe and anywhere in the world.

My expressions in this book are unfiltered, sincere, and channeled into a medium called, "poetry", under the sub genre: "free verse". In other words, I did what I felt like doing, said what I felt like saying, blah, blah; to thine own self be true. (smile) I am so thankful that you have tuned in to my distortion and perceptions of the truth (as only God is the supreme truth). We only see [*love*] in part but one day it will all be made clear. *(1 Corinthians 13:12)*

In this book, I've written about some of the complex emotions (not necessarily situations) that people that I care for and I have experienced. What I've come to learn through writing these poems and facing the conditions I (at the time) chose is that all of our choices are affected by the way we feel about ourselves and the beliefs we adapt. It [writing this book] taught me that it is so important to have a healthy idea of who we are so that we can choose better for our lives.

I've attempted to capture the perceptions (blind/broken/beloved) while they existed and put them in a book. I've done so in the simplest way I knew how, from my point of view, through poetry. I promise to never speak above you, or down to you. This book does serve earthly good. I do not want to lose you in the environment of my art, nor in the momentum of my emotions as we artist tend to do that. I want to share my, then, insight and feelings with you. No matter the condition you are in when this book finds you (blind/broken/beloved), know that we are on the same page, even as you turn the page; and we are on even ground, even as we excel in life.

When you decide to read *Based On A Love Story*, my hope is that you will be able to take these entries in with an open heart and mind. Poetry should be read with your heart “eyes”, not your physical eyes or even your brain “eyes” (to some degree). Because oddly enough, I have found some of the best things I’ve expressed where when I felt like I was out of my mind and all in my feelings. It’s the only way it [poetry] will make sense. My hope is that these poems are easy to receive and digest. Metaphorically speaking, I want you to eat them until you are full, they are chocked full of *love*; purposely so, and, all intended to make you burp. (smile) Some will require you chew on it for a minute, chop it up and take it in smaller portions, others digest best through sipping. But of your favorite of the collection you'll slurp, gobble, devour, and return for more. So long as you are fed, my purpose is served. (smile)

My *love* language is best expressed through writing. I did a lot of soul searching while being guided to create this book. Trust and believe me when I say we share in the discomforts, and embarrassments with the honesty in a lot of these poems. It is not easy taking a look at who you were or how you once thought, but it is such a breath of fresh air to see who you are and what you are becoming. I put "I *love* you" in my willingness to understand others, to share, to relive and to rescue anyone that may have had a hard time *loving* themselves as I once did. Getting through heart ache (of any kind) can be quite difficult, but becoming aware of who we are, what *love* truly is; our Creator, offers a peace that passes all understanding. I am not perfect in the least, but I am still striving, daily, towards Him and striving to become a better woman.

I hope that this book inspires you in every way possible to be the fullest expression of your potential on this Earth. I hope it sets you free from bondage. I hope that you enjoy my gift to you. Most importantly, I hope that you choose *love*, now and always.

I am truly blessed to be with you in Spirit, in Heart and in Mind.

Love *always*,

Danielle

:BLIND:

7 Days Before Valentine's Day

without your permission pieces of you were stolen
tiny segments of great appreciation for you
were all tucked away deep inside a place
that can be accessed at my will

i added these segments to cherished memories
it was while you slept that
the vision of these eyes retrieved:
the climatic curl in the upper part of your lip
the dusty lazy sweep of your brow
the bold respectful bowing in the bridge of your nose
the gentle blend of your almond color
the brown textures of your black skin

the vision of these eyes
took liberties with the new hair sprouting round your edge up
and now its all etched in my brain
like the tattoo in your upper arm
and since you always forward the photos of you that i have taken
and distribute them along with your parts to other women
i can't share these thoughts with you
cause neither you nor them would internalize it as i do
and to protect my ego
there will be no hard proof of me being a fool for you

A Letter To Daddy

i wanted to ask you why you left.
many times i have wanted to ask you to stay but
if mommy was not enough to compel you than what were we?

there were nights we stayed alone
in the three bedroom home and
before than
i had gotten so used to laying in your arms at night
back in the big city we had come from
and moved from
without you...

there were six of us
and we had four beds
and they were twins so their one bed, bunked
and he had his own and the older two had theirs and
since i always just preferred being up under you and mommy
i, bed-less,
slept with
whomever would welcome me in their sheets
never knowing i had created an appetite
of bed jumping, looking for you:
a man
i can still count them on one hand
at a time
but daddy
i was just missing you so bad
and all the times we had
demolishing Danish sugar cookies
and watching baseball games together
you loved the Yankee's
they were the only team in the world to you
and New York City the only place in the world for me
as long as i could be with you and
i always thought your scent was a type of cologne
and its no wonder the attraction i have to men that
carry the aroma of rum on their breath
still i would claim you shameless, always, none the less...

ask me and i would tell anyone -
imperfections and all, you were the best

anyway
i don't know where you are
i have written this letter many times since grade school
always rewriting a new one every year because i was never happy to send you
my undeveloped hand script
and even as an adult
i still can't mature into my vulnerability quite right and just say
i need you
not for your money or for your status but
there is something
missing

and its something that seems essential
that would have never been if you had never been
i couldn't be here without you...it takes two
so what makes you think i can live without you
she couldn't conceive me on her own
what idea could you fathom or conjure that would convince you
she could raise us alone?
i mean i have made it here fine
to some degree
but i could have made it here
faster and with less scraps on my knees
from praying so much or not enough,
but instead begging
some janky nigga to do what you never would
or didn't figure out how to
love me
you still win
i am still unable to send it and address it to some recipient
from an address with no location in particular
because i am still kind of lost
for words like i've been for many years now
so i'll make the paper pay the debts and the ink to grieve under the pressure
i can make the unscripted stuff legible from my heart

daddy
i really just wanted your smile
the smell of your skin

the security of your embrace
the reassurance of your presence
the honesty in your laughter
the command of your voice
and though
mommy has sworn it many years before about you
...you *ain't all that*
i beg to differ

a little girl always knows
her daddy is the king of everything
and i know that's so
Walt Disney of me to believe but
i wish that of all the false "hoods" that you convinced me
to build a castle inside of
i wished that you being "superman" was one of them
you didn't have to be capable of doing everything
i just wanted you to do any thing...
that meant everything
to me

A Poem About The Invisible Man

its hard to believe
a man exist that finds joy in loving me
finds joy in greeting my forehead with a morning kiss
one that takes the time to admire my smile
its hard to believe
a man exist that could fall in love with
and not pick apart every imperfect detail in my oral cavity.

i'm struggling for the faith
and hope of knowing he can feel me on the inside
and find places in my soul
not readily exposed
that he would labor to search places where my fears and doubts
hold hostage, my happiness, at gun point.
so i keep my mouth shut - even a fish knows how
i don't want to get hooked up on no man's crooked dick
and tossed back in the sea, salty.
who would want to drown in bitterness,
unable to surface for fresh air?
that alone would be hard to swallow.
or better yet be left ashore gasping to be in my rightful place
...praying for God, again, *can you help me*
he took me out of my element.

who wants the dark complexion?
no one visits the other side of moon
the shadow from the light
the minimal of light - societies stigma of all things 'bad'.
someone has got to know the value of onyx
even when my daddy wasn't as insightful enough to know it

it's almost as if they can see through this gemstone
don't they recognize the pressures that form diamonds?
no one drills for me, no one digs deep.
i must blend in with the dirt that molds me
i'm so afraid to be "me"
nothing about "her" must interest 'em.
so she keeps "her" mouth shut.
and "she" knows men fall in love with what they see.

and "she" knows what they want
and "she" knows on occasion what she needs
but someone now has got to teach me.
someone has got to teach me that its okay to be loved
even if i have no idea how to
and even if i've never even seen it
towards me
and that only makes its hard to believe
a man can exist that finds joy in loving me.

A Poem For A Love Transitioned

(for Daddy, B-Luv, David, EttaMae, Neo Abyss & all those we loved & lost)

i hope that when i sing out loud
it reaches you in heaven
with the angels and God.
i will shine
even will i shine
in the darkest hours of my nights like a star
just to get close to where you are
with the angels and God

there isn't a day that visits
that doesn't invite you with remembrance
loving you was never an option i had
it came without question
inclined to do so
privileged to have had the opportunity
i could gather the birds of the air
from every hemisphere and from every pocket of sky
the world has ever known
and in unison
they could not mimic the cries of my pain
i still feel you with me
though its like a dream now believing you ever existed
its easier that way to imagine life in the natural sense without you
as a dream

you were my breath of fresh air
supply cut short
how my life has not ended without oxygen
i do not know
in all that i do
if it can resonate higher in some frequency
beyond what i see
its with great hopes

that when i sing out loud
it reaches you in heaven

with the angels and God
i will shine
even will i shine
in the darkest hours of my nights
like you, my star
just to get close to where you are
with the angels and God

Black Butterfly (You've Changed)

black butterfly
you were never designed to be an eagle
but still you fly
the sky is the limit
stop here

there are no higher heights for you to climb
nothing exist for you beyond this here-sphere
you are warned: "danger lurks there"
it would be in your best interest to stay low
stay underneath a glass ceiling
and imagine how wonderful it would be to
taste the butter of the churning sun

it may appear from afar that even the sparrow gets a sample of its richness
and everyone knows that every blade of grass looks greener from the other side.
weightless like a feather of the bird that you envy
the bird that would be your devourer
if you climb higher

it would be nice
if and only if
you black butterflies
could join together against the prey that eats you
but
you are only granted 24 hours to enjoy your limited life
so you refuse sacrificing life for any another creature
just as black just as similar
just as weak as you are
i can not judge you for that choice
as we're all guilty of squeezing
gluttonous ways into the starving codes
of survival modes

black butterfly
you opted to take pleasure in your day
gliding along the winds
that if turned torrent would without question
shred your wings to pieces
but you're living for yourself

and you're dying for yourself
and what would your life be worth
if you could not choose what to die for?

black butterfly
i see you

made to fly
never too high
you've been warned *not to forget that*
and yet still you fly

audacious like a speckled dots on a rainbow of colorful flowers
across a meadow of lilies, daisies, chrysanthemums, and tulips.
you are like black pepper on tropical fruit.
you are out of place, yet perfect in your imperfection
intriguing to the eye, inquisitive to the senses
too distinguished a taste to digest
without something to neutralize your flavor

you are out of place,
so i've been told
like every other black thing in this world

black butterfly
you are a tiny angel
no origin of your color, gender
selfless in your purpose
selfish in your pursuit
dancing along the colors of the field
yearning to blend in their togetherness
ultimately rejecting you from the color scheme
a scheme you weren't let in on
an inability to camouflage with the garden
and it feels like betrayal to your life that it isn't so
just black makes more black
just 'original' some say
just 'nothing' others think
but just a "you" to be embraced

if we trace the outline of your wings diagonally

we'll discover
two overlapping signs of infinity
yet a life so delicate, finite

the weightless bird
that sings a silent song
offers no contribution to the pattern of the wind
no resistance against the push of the air
you are but a decoration an ornament to the flow of air

but unlike any other creature
you did change from what you were:
metamorphosis
something that even in our evolutionary
human *elite-ness*
we are reluctant to do.
crawling on your belly to be who you are today
even in your humility
i admire you
because
you came higher

Cookie Cutter

he scouted her for talent
though she won't no girl scout
saw her coke bottle shape
and went after her cookies
innocently
like a child he came
foolishly
she loosened the lid
for him to reach in the jar.
she shared her delectable treat
he smashed and scattered
every part of her to crumbs.
her heart crumbled like dust
he blew her hopes into the wind
like dandelion pods
she wasn't tough enough
had her wide open strung stupid.
he told his boys
she was his favorite type
"tagalong"

Couching Crotch, Invisible Snake

it was foolish to sit there, skin wet
waiting on your call.

crotch damp, mouth dry, eyes peered, palms gripping
waiting on your call.
body hot, shower cold, rain pouring
waiting on your call.

chest swelled, mind less, and void of intelligence,
waiting on your call.
wanting to be licked not a lick of sense.
but waiting on your call.

heart pounding in my ears,
body all contorted,
house quiet and ghost of our massacred love
tiptoeing on the floor of my bedroom
haunting the limbs of my body
screaming down the halls of my heart
and waiting on your call.

it was foolish to settle as a "confidant"
and not with a title.
women never fall for childish games.

i haven't learned yet.
i haven't learned yet.
but i will learn, i will learn today

how to be a woman.
and i will learn
what momma taught me long ago
"a stiff dick has no sympathy"
and that made it easy
for you to tell me you were falling in love with me,
and me to make it okay to for you to lie to her and lie with me
the other lovely lady.

Declaration of Dependence

i want to say how i feel; bet you would only laugh at me.
declarations to the world; bet they would only laugh at me.
i got my heart underneath my arms, clutched tight in a choke hold.
always wrestling, i'm always wrestling.

i want to tell you it aches, the way it presses my chest
only short of breath -
so its better to back away to get room to breathe.
i could call it love - four letters to a word
with endless ways to define it.

and until i have become something familiar with the etymology
i don't want to confess that either.
i know i've been wrong before.
i know when i'm right, i'm right as i can be.

been right `bout this just once in my life
but that was only when realizing that i should learn to love me.
its like my auntie June say,
"aw hell,"

well what about you? i
...really don't know about you...
i know i got "me" on guarantee all day
from sun up to sun down
everything outside me's an uncertainty.

yes
i should consider that you live in my heart
no vacancies
and as an assumed rule
that makes you a part of me
it was not guarded so that makes it free territory.

and since all is fair in this war called love:
i deny my heart any bit of useless sense
with the fear that acknowledging what i feel about you
confessed or confined
is killing me

First Love

when my pockets were stuffed full of lint
you generously emptied the ones of your heart
and gave to me love that i've never known,
first.
i loved you first.
top priority, first.

our first kiss
pressed upper and bottom lips
was that of one mouth,
before i met you i longed for you
i knew before i met you that when these tears fell into
the corners of my mouth
you tasted them where ever you were
and then you came and found me.
we loved each other.

i've always hated our goodbyes
even when i understood them as a lesson.
you are still a wonder to behold when i make music in the form of words
like Stevie does
i trace a ribbon laced in the sky inscribed
and the banner says: "love was here".
i still find you in songs
they will always be ours
even after the hearing loss
when we've fallen deaf to our broken promises
to love each other forever

the songs
i still hear them as a message from you to i
it serves as a reminder that you loved me once.
there will always remain in my pupils
a partial blindness for you.
i still fumble to find the right chords to strike a nerve
in the harp of my heart strings again
while in search of a new angel.
no one strummed as skillfully as you.

even if you once patronized me saying that i act as if i

'wrote the book on love'.
called me a know it all
dismissed me and i thought you a hypocrite for saying so
because you were the template,
the catalyst, the model, the image,
the statue, statute, the stature
font, ink, calligraphy, impression, indention and muse
that inspired it, if indeed i had written it.
with love as the topic -
you were everything
i've
ever needed
to know.

so now i have written a book about love,
not all about it
but like the Bible says
only: in part.
i guess i can say now
"i told you so" or you can say it,
or we could adjust your foot into your mouth
and i hope your heart accepts that last line
as a reason to smile.
because i loved you once.
and i've always hated being wrong
even if i wasn't the right one for you

someone else loves you now
the spirit of love towards you
has ascended from me and has rested in their bosom;
so my words must be tender towards you and in order, the thank you's,
for the lesson in true fidelity extended with pure intent.
and i hope that where ever living angels greet you
the hands of your mind fold the corners of this particular poem
and you hold it near, dear
and tuck it back into those pockets of your heart that you once emptied for me.

we thought we were each other's "one"
but since it was not you
nor could it have been me
i pray you embrace this part of me
entirely in the form of poetry.

i promised i would tell the world i did
love you
and though i had not the vehicle or platform then
i kept my word now.
this is to you, a first love, a homage;
knowing that i will never forget the experience of loving
and being loved by you.

Help Me Reach

i bet.
if i close my eyes tight enough
and make daylight black
i ain't got to face reality
seeing what i think i saw, or maybe stay blind to it
i can ignore the "hints"
like maybe, it won't matter at the end of the day

it makes me sick though.
how i take you back every time
after these big issue i it minimize to
small issues
here and there
tiny like dust particles that make me sneeze

even small things add up to big ones
and dust turns to clumps of dirt
and dirt covers the grave

maybe i should question if this will ultimately
bury me alive if i don't walk away
and if it does
would it be considered
martyrdom?

love is self sacrificing

i don't want this to die
and i don't want to be buried in
"concerns" and "doubts" and "what ifs"
cause it feels like i'd die without you
chances are, i know, i'll survive
ten times out of ten.

but i'll be dead [on the inside]
and they'll be no resurrecting
again, what we call love
cause i can't just be "friends"
the
irony that i hope its not toxic

to have you around in such a capacity.

i could do nothing lesser then to lower my
expectations
standard
for you so that you can get through
to the heaven i want to give you
and perhaps my heart
the heart i want you to fit in

so i fall to my knees
in faith
right here
and here in prayer
i can stand ten feet tall - reaching on your behalf

UP

to hope floating high over our heads.

hopes are high

we don't have to drown here if only you would
help me reach

Imaginary Friend

imaginary Friend

not supposed to tell you bout my imaginary friend
cause imaginary friends supposed to be a secret

i see my friend, and my friend sees you
but you don't see them...and we see each other
and when you don't see us
me and my friend play games that we keep secret

we play games that will get me spanked
and my imaginary friend knows i hate that

so i can't tell you what the game is
or when we play
or that i learned to like it
...like all things that feel good

at least i ain't getting spanked

not supposed to tell you bout my imaginary friend

or that my friend makes it okay to take off my shorts
and run around in my ruffled panties when you are gone

and out my shirt cause it got too hot to play in
i could take off everything if i wanted to

but my friend wanted me to
...so i did
cause i like when they smile and
i know smiling at me means i am doing it right

and my friend laughed and played with me.

tickles my belly with their imaginary fingers
and kiss the little dark dots on my chest
the friend is imaginary
but i feel it

i feel it for real, mommy

i used to cry when my friend touched me
but to make me feel better
they let me know i ain't in trouble
gives me candy when your gone
small gifts when you're looking mommy
so you can trust them too like i trust them

...my friend makes noises
when they press my brown dark chest dots
like horns...
"honk! honk!" not too loud though
might wake someone and our game will end

they say that to me...
i laugh...cause its fun to me now
now that it's a game
then i touch theirs like i am told to
i make noises too
"beep beep..."
my friend laughs and...closes...his...eyes slowly...

and then i get a kiss on the mouth

i'm not supposed to tell you because it's a secret

my friend showed me the flap between my lil legs
and how to make that lump of skin stiff...
and when my friend is gone i always rub on it...
cause sometimes its stiff when my friend it gone
...and
you see me
...and
you slap my hands away
and you won't make the stiff stop
and all you say is
"you only 5 years old you shouldn't be touching down there no how..."

maybe its a kiddie thing

...cause little girls not supposed to do that...

you tell me not to touch it.
but my imaginary friend allowed to, right?
and you do it too when you bathe me
so *only* grown ups… only grown ups can touch me there

okay, got it.

my imaginary friend is all grown up
so they ain't got to ask permission

only i see my friend
and they see you
and you don't see them…
but we always see each other

but i ain't supposed to tell you where they at
my friend says it's a game…and this game
is our little secret

Inspiration (dedicated to those that idolize the sweetest frame)

let's hold hands.
we should hold hands
cause it is inadvertently
conveniently where i house my heart

and i can't help but adore what they touch

and the matters of my heart are within these hands
and this is where i put my insides on a page
and it is through these hands that i bare my soul

i have never been good with origami
but i make one hell of a body of work
on a sheet of paper with ink
i am not God
but to be able to create He bestowed upon me a generous
portion of that aspect of His image.
i am a creator

and if i touch you with my hands
that makes you special
to me
you may feel like dirt
but i will touch you with these hands
and breathe life into you with my kiss
i will make you come alive
i will use my words and breathe life into you for all of the readers
so that you will be found on record
the tallest of men mightiest in your ways
bolder in your strengths
blood of my sweat and the sweat of my tears
you are my inspiration

so i am careful
i am careful with whom
i share my
body

and with every knot dented in my knuckles

fingers
from root to narrow tip,
i am inspired by you
that makes you
special to me
and with both of my hands
muscles of my palms
possessed jerk of my wrist
i etch as an artist
and sketch in freelance
my depiction of you
through ink
through angular stroke
through fluid motion
through tight bend
masterfully

and that
in itself
makes you
special to me

Lament

i wish i could save you family
i wish i could reach my arms down, deep down
into the flames of hell where you have made your bed
where you lay
woman with woman
woman with man
man with woman
man with man

liquor hugging doubts
tears intimate with fear
blade coaxing wrist
strange dick penetrating vagina
husband to adulterous woman
cheater of a man
closed fisted abuse to soft female flesh
pride to hard ego
outright lies to bitter hate
back biting and backstabbing
and wake you up, shake you up.
i wish i could show you goodness and all that's in store
i wish i could bring back fruit from the promise land
big enough to fill more than enough of your appetite
i wish i could let you sip how refreshing and cleansing it is
to wash the dirt from the walls of your heart
the dirt from your hands; the blood from your hands
and break the chains off the ankles of your soul
and just let you run free.

i wish you could love again
and breath again
and just let you be YOU again.
not the you that you think you ought to be for everybody
but the YOU that is more comfortably... real, and honestly you.
not "standing your ground" you
the reason you were "born" you
and help you forget the "*because of the hurt*" you

i wish the devil didn't have a toe or foothold in your threshold
in your home, in your food

in the bread you break
that you feed to the children; that you eat
that you make a part of you when you digest...
cause it only makes you full of that
brown, stink and

i wish i could save you...
from all that, excuse my profanity, shit.

i wish i could strip the blurriness from your pupils
and slide these rose tints on your eyes
and i wish things were still beautiful to you
i wish that i could raise you up out of these small and insignificant issues
that make a world of difference to you
sit you on top of the world and let you know when you are ready
it is yours for the taking.

i wish when you looked in the mirror
it was with the eyes of God to see in you what He placed in you...
i am not Jesus Christ...i am so imperfect...
but if only He could work mightily through me

then i could save you.
cause through Him that would be possible
like all things are supposed to be

its possible... its possible...its possible.
i will save you

No Words To Say

i tried to see you on the blank page before i wrote this.
but love is blind,
i got to feel my way through these feelings
only to find the words:
braille
braille for a dialog and
braille for a script and
braille that ain't phonetically assigned to my lips...
and the inexplicable that lead my pen to speak.
i can't form the words, i don't know how to say
...sorry... when you aren't happy.
because that's all you deserve and all i want you to be.
i find myself unhappy until you are.
in any other case i am lost if i can't share your joy
or for that matter if you have none.
i know you aren't happy with me
i've been changing all that i could
since it seems a privilege to me to make you happy.
i can't control the variables of being unlucky should they ever strike our lives
beautifully patterned and if it leaves us torn apart.
if i could be the perfect me,
the perfect financial structure, provider and giver, the perfect
smile and frame and body and mind
and minus the irregularities
attitudes and polarities
and if i could be refined gold instead of raw findings
i'd do what i could and fashion it for you beautifully
as you've been for me.
i would be something like
a display on a runway and model every part sequentially.
all in the proceeding order
i want the strength
i want the ammunition
i want the courage
to be all you need

She Needs A Daddy

if he were a father to her
her feet would not find cold streets to pace
in search for one.

if he knew well enough to inspire her
with *upliftings* and *informings* towards her
and with urgency of her beauty
her flesh would not crave the caress
of a strangers hands to tell her.

nor would her flesh justify the abuse of her lover
as her acceptance of the abuse
is an unspoken agreement to her belief that
she is hideous and she deserves this.

if he understood that
love had everything to do with it
she would not be slighted by the distractions of her mother
looking for a replacement
because he failed to love even the woman
she favored.

if he had counted the cost of the worth of a warm embrace
she would not be so persuaded to believe
that men were incapable of housing love in their hearts
and maybe in her bitterness
she would not have limited love to existing in the same sex.

if he considered his very own power
he would have known it wasn't the value of the dollars that
he lacked but the presence of his worth and existence
that she would have treasured most.

but instead he ran
and that little girl needs a daddy
to teach her the type of man that contributes to life
in the proper sense
not just in the sense of popping one in her.

she needs a daddy to make it clear that a rise in the crotch

does not guarantee a rise in the heart of a man,
or his rise to an occasion to be a man of valor.

if he could understand that his daughter needs his love
she could raise the sons and choose the brilliant and brave fathers
to raise the sons and end a vicious cycle
of a dysfunctional family.

imagine that as a trend

Spoils Of War

i will not be a spoil of war.
"war" interchangeable with "love"
as in it, they say, "all's fair".

not sure who "they" are
though i quote them often.

but if it is true,
if "they" have any credentials;

i would be a third world country
unequipped at this time for battle
struck by guerrilla warfare tactics
raped of her harvest
starving in search of rations
needing strong allegiances
and a true ally to fight
by my side.

The Asscuse: Why I could Not Write The Love Song

they asked me to write a *love* song.
i had the lead, i had no point.
and i guess that was for the best
because even with the right words
there would be nothing much to sing about.
there would be nothing much to say,
there would be nothing much to recite
there would be nothing much to rehearse,
and i would still have no part to play even if there was.

there is no song of my expression
and there is no truth i need to expel.
i don't know how to spell *love* without tilting the letters out of place
awkward spaces non-legible script.

seems so foreign to me and odd to pronounce
like a new language without the confidence to speak to a native.
i missed the days that i was unconscious
dreaming of this thing that i was in, but not really in
i was in the fog alone and didn't realize 'til i woke up
that i was holding my own hand leading myself to hopes and dreams of another
that failed to reflect anything equal.

and we all know a broken mirror is bad luck
for how ever many years
we leave the fragments on the ground to cut us.
so i picked up my pieces
and bandaged up my soft crack creases and figured
it's better to hurt in reality
instead of bumping into everything blindly
superficially
and not even know i was bruised.

I took my turn at being dumb,
so numb to everything but a fluttering in my gut.
until it started to hurt

now i am numb to the pain
and love isn't a sharp enough point to pierce a heart once its calloused.

point noted.

i used that line in a four line stanza once
but my brain froze and i went back at it.
i swear
even if i should not have, not by heaven or a hair

i had writer's block about this *love* thing
i got locked out
until i locked myself in
and swallowed the first key that set me free
i still feel imprisoned.
i still feel inadequate.
i still feel dumb.
even after i learned *love* don't love me
and maybe learning what i thought i knew won't even right at all.
they asked me to sing a *love* song
but i didn't hit the notes right
at least not when i tried
i ain't got the voice for it
and my momma said i can't sing no how.
don't nobody listen to me sang,
even in the shower with that natural reverb
or peering from the curtains of my silhouette's shadow,
even when i pour my heart out
and i still don't know what to do `bout these broken promises i'm holding on to
cause the tighter i hold
the more they slip between my fingers

i said forget it...
and i can't read sheet music.
they said my voice was the instrumental
now i'm going mental
i've sung this melody before
screeching like a skinned cat
skipping like a broken record.

i have been flipped upside down
a switch: turned on to be a turn off.
i tried using the rhythm of my life and my heart
as the beat of my drum to march alone
and not in sync with anyone or thing but only

found myself in a sink
down a drain where i washed all the yoke...
for being unequally yoked.
that's what i get putting all my eggs in the hand basket
the one i tucked myself inside on the ride to hell
cause that is what *love* felt like when it burned.
....they wanted me to sing a *love* song but
they didn't like it cause it just won't pretty.

didn't want it because after i sung it
the song won't giddy
and they won't clapping no more
and they ain't smiling no more.
'cause all their joy is gone,
i tried to make it as real as i could,
but they wanted me to fake it
wanted to pretend it was so easy and so fun
so colorful when
singing...
them kind of blues.
i ain't into lying.
never been good at it.
i just don't sing that kind of song right.

The Children

out of the mouths of babes the truth spins
silk worms and woven thread
something far more delicate
than adult minds
can comprehend

the pure fabric within the youth
has the potential to be
piled layer upon layer
a thick blanket of comfort that
protects and provides
warmth far more sustainable
than adult hands are
in their maturity
willing to extend to their peers
equals and brethren

so explain the self degrading, all fours to floor
dogging them out
barking at angels as dogs to pest
or clawing the walls of their hearts with doubts
are these cats serious?

or using iron fist to seize control
of their limitless potential
because as an adult
they're upset that they allow another
adult to limit their own.

there is no monster
under a child's bed
larger than the hateful words
a parent can plant into their heads

What You Do To Me (For the love of Music)

sometimes
you are like a man i am unsure of
and i feel idiotic for feeling for you what i feel for you.
i put everything on the line for you.
i can't get close enough to you from here
makes me want to run away
makes me want to hide away.
i got to find another way.
i tried to feel for someone, anyone else what i feel for you.
my love ain't perfect, but i'm trying to be a better facilitator.
damn
i should be embarrassed
- everyone is watching...
questioning the obsession...like
"really...look at you...you think that's gonna happen?"
...they say i ain't good enough for you
i ain't pretty enough for you, that i don't deserve you.
i got so much hope in our potential that i eliminate all the options.
i've been crying myself to sleep about this
i feel so weak about this.
thought i knew it before, thought i knew it once...
but i wonder if you will keep the promises you make to me.
please love me like i love you.
i knew it was love
the first time i felt you run through me
the first time i heard you.
every action of yours like a mirror image i mimic.
i'm trying to get like you.
i want so much to be like you.
see so much of me in you... i can't get over it...
and i got to fight for it.
got to tell ya, if i don't have you, its like i'll die

what would i do with out you music?
what would i do without my dream?

this desire and this passion
no one hears me like you.
and no one hears you like me.

i wish i could place my thoughts on their hearts
and minds like i do this page...
wish i was free to say it all.
but you have been my easel.
you never withheld from me what i struggled to never withhold from you.
your spirit and the truth of what you are on so many levels.
i want you to understand me
and i want us to show the world our chemistry
and i need you to open your arms to me, music.
i need you to show me what true love is & i need us to
show the world what pure love is...
cause if i can't find it on earth's surface...
i'll devote my love to my
music, music,
....music.

Wildflower (for the wildflowers of the world)

since yo' roots is so deep i guess you just gonna stand yo' ground.
nobody tamed you, can't nobody touch you.
don't nobody want to pluck and store you away on the side of their bed
only beautiful to watch from afar.
he wants you in his garden
but he just don't know how to handle you.
cause you a Wildflower
and he knows that even if he wanted to gather roses
he would still find a briar patch of thorns guarding her beauty
baby you make it so easy
you still invite the bees for honey
and the nectars always so sweet
always so free.
and they take, and taste
and where you share your interior
is unlike the places on the exterior
no spikes in yo' center, though they ought to be.
you will not be moved.
cause yo' roots too deep
in the earth you stand
and you just gonna stick with standing your ground

wildflower
you are deemed to be beautiful
but nobody wants to keep you for nothing more than looking, sniffing
plucking, tossing into the fire
you've got to save your petals from being plucked,
other wise
you'll be a useless center ovary,
exposing your ovule
full of foreign pollinated seeds
and you deserve to be mentioned
when they teach the life lesson on nature
and about all the pretty birds
and about all the ambitious bees

Work Clothes (Labor of Love)

tears ain't nothing but liquid hangers
displaying my countenance through the windows
of my soul.
i may be draped in sadness, with a petticoat covering of despair
and the heart on my sleeve fragile like a faberge pendant;
but they'll still be rolled up and I'll still be elbow deep
giving 100% to our love.

Womanhood (part 1)

one day
like all the women i've read about
and admired
- the Aretha's, the Jill's, the Lauryn's, the Mary's,
the Coretta's, the Toni's, the Nikki 's-
i will be able to make this *thang*
look so easy
one day
my hair won't fall out of place
my body won't feel so awkward
and i won't have to apologize for my dips
full lips and wide hips
swings and turns and pivots
and the Earth will just have to sit patiently
hands folded in its lap
and wait while i stride from point A to point B
cause C ...
one day
some young girl will ask me
in admiration
how to be confident and i will tell her
boldly, that it's a *choice*
like discipline
its a muscle that you must exercise
to become stronger
i, by then
i would know confidence like the back of my very own hand

guess i should accept
that its just like what i wanted at some time
when my front was as flat as my back
a set of lush breast
womanhood will show up when it's good and damn ready
and with such *grandeur*
and i will have to make the proper adjustments
womanhood will be here when i feel unprepared for it
and be as forceful and painful at its arrival as something i didn't want
a period
thought it: *womanhood*

would just show up one morning with all my ducks paddling in a row
it has not been so
only coming to find she is like everything else
something that must be developed with every instance and
long suffering
the adage has proven itself true, that age is but a number
and 18 plus don't mean a thang
one day
these little boys and their idiot behavior might not appeal to my interest
as of this moment, i still haven 't discovered a way to say no
and mean it
without answering the call hoping he'll apologize
feeling like *'if he leaves I lose everything'*
or giving him another chance when he hasn't grown into deserving one
and maybe i'll find her in sincere friendships with females
that do not need to compete
or pretend
or complain
females whose yes are their yes
whose no's are their no's
and i will not shy away from my potential
in fear of being hated
maybe she is behind the heart ache and heartbreak i am headed for
maybe she has foresight to walk away from disaster
because i am such a childish foolish girl
i can not say no without considering someone's hurt feelings
maybe she will come when i can set boundaries
when i am brave enough to seize my territory.
one day
i will know her
capture and own her
and make this *thang*
look so easy

⁝ BROKEN ⁝

Connotation: Frienemy

what are frienemies?

frienemies. noun.
a shell of skin, void of heart, void of consideration.
paper thin, feather light – changing directions with the change of the wind.
people, persons, folk of interest that wear titles – wear wool as the preferred item of clothes.

"sheep" clothing is their favorite brand name
until they soil them and discard them,
and trade their couture for snake skin
and wear these new suits and make it seem as if
this is the way it is…
this is who i always was –
and this is the way it must be.
then got the nerve to say,
"i thought you knew me…"

always covering their asses,
and in the end minimizes your sincere loving kindness…
to stupidity.
kind of feels like you're the ass for extending a hand
… and upon exposing the naked truth…
learning that they were wolves all along

their negative convictions towards you
can only cause you to request they stick by them
when the tables turn to your favor
as no false agenda will work for them
any longer

they accuse you of flawed intent
as their own heart confessions
based on their own belief systems
they want to use you
to carry them and

…this has become a common truth:
that they [frienemies] will bite you

so don't feed them.

what are frienemies?
smile in your face, text behind your back via blackberry
and the berry they once extended you plucked
and you ate
and it made
you blue
as fruits from bad trees will often do
as bad fruit is what bad trees produce.

being absent of heart
in the presence of your company
like a sound barrier
blocks what you hear; what you feel what you know,
but you stay around and you trust and you
pray it ain't so...

what are frienemies?

people, persons, folk of interest that form alliances against you
breed familiarity –
breed contempt, breed hatred, breed envy and agree to resent you.

what are frienemies?
people, persons, folk of interest that select you out of convenience;
comfortable with being walking contradictions
never accepting your imperfections – remain long enough that you build their confidence
their strength, their ego: they leave you
drained

they leave you weak.
to the top, they will openly doubt is that place that you go
they leave you hung over like too much liquor
and dehydrated, never watering the seeds of your potential
they leave you sick to your stomach.
they leave you.

After The Blow

sometimes
it's too much.
i look around within a world that lives happily
without me...

and question why i am here.

i wonder what happened to the warmth i felt
for those that should feel for me
i wonder if i am
disposable

or if they think me
dangerous...
they won't get close to me.

and in turn, i will not be close to them.

sometimes,
the flavor of lonely is so bitter
and heavy
i try to bury it
with sweets, lots of them...
it mixes like citrus and milk -
both are too much;

so i vomit them.
and flush them.
and hope it all disappears – never to return again.

by then my throat is burning
and words don't come forward easily.
but my heart knows

i want to be understood – without forcing anyone to understand
because i go – even without the fuel to push me – the extra mile
to understand them.

why did they leave me?

it's the question i ask.

and where do we go from here?
is the next one that follows…

and alone now, i ask
where do i go from here?
since you are no longer here to help me through this betrayal
because you inflicted these wounds

no one of them wants to give me the secret to survive,
but every one of them secretly plots to destroy me.

after the blow, after the tears: i look in the mirror
at the face that was there since birth,
sentenced to life with me
and i ask myself "if it does…"

the same question the rest of them ask me…
"…hurt"

like i ain't got no
fucking feelings.

my answer is always the same, and has yet to change
"...i can't afford for it to…"

thinking…i may have too much to lose if ever feelings do
and i lift my baggage on my back,
in bags that just may contain the weight of the world
life goes on, with or without me...
...or with them...

and i keeps it moving…
and its not always because i want to,

i move on because i have to.

Angry

when you open your mouth
all those words that weighed so heavily
fly over my head
as hollow, weightless things will tend to do

you see how you do?

with the betrayal and lies?
how is that any way to compromise?
that is no way to remain on terms good
when you got bad intentions

you are not so stupid
as you portray your ways to be
you are not without vision as you can not see
you make me evil.
you make my pure heart dirty.
you make me sinister.
you make my sincerity a sin.

its going to be worse now
for anyone after
burn in hell
the way you burned my heart
the way my eyes burned when you made me cry
the way the tender skin burned and began to swell
the way the mascara ran from my lashes
the way it burned when you ran to her
the way the truth burned
while it sunk in to every layer
every strand and fiber to the core of this love
inside of my being for you
the way it singed the boarders of my life
and left me exposed
i was everyone joke
only included in the punch-line

i'm an open wound now
all sorts of parasites are entering into my psyche:
the pathogens killing the idea that true love will ever be mine

the microbe of anguish
shakes me out of my sleep with fever
the virus of loneliness
the cancer of hatred
eating me up inside;

never ever thought
i would want someone to die,
but that is what i get
doing my own thinking
leaning on to my own understanding
and i am thinking my own
contradiction now:
and you can both rot
in the lowest parts of hell

Anxiety of Alone

you were so uninvited
no one invited you in here.
came barging in, awkward and dilapidated ...
i hate this moment.

you always seem to reserve your visits upon my rising
morning after mourning.
souring on my stomach and escorted with anxiety
and blowing air into these lonely wounds

how arrogant are you to cradle my jugular vein with the fangs of regrets
how vicious are you to claw at my throat and choke me with tears?
loneliness is bleeding me empty

bleeding me empty of all the joys
i have yet and not promised the luxury to experience.
how familiar it has become to me
the loathsome sensation of separation.

separation from a kindred spirit i have yet to encounter.
whose going to love me?
how damning a condemnation are the tones and resonating lows in the voice of solitude

it always screams out, its always echoing in the chambers of my heart
its always been a cold world outside these walls of my dwelling place -
and the reality that there is no one to love.

how then can i call this a "home"?
or find comfort in this rest?
my bed sheets are like insulation pads surrounding my stone cold heart

i am trapped between these sheets
and this mattress; a cave floor for stalagmites.
i am frost bitten, deprived of the warmth of love.
whose going to hold me?
whose going to want me?
whose going to love me?

Appetite Suppressant

it may take months, years
books with colorful characters, legendary heroes;
semesters in a new field;
new regional foods in a different state
winds of a Midwestern city;
strict laws in a commonwealth, providence;
a foreign country with bi-linguistics;
a conquest of personal defeat;
Webster and his catalog of vocabulary
before the tip of this pen can excavate the words
rooted into this rotted cavity of a heart.

but i will find a way to communicate the hell that i'm burning inside of by being with you

if only i could land some place
zero in on this from a new height, a higher level;
expand the parachute of my mind,
further and wider beyond the tiny skies of this world
of hatred you've trapped us in.

the pain is so paralyzing that my future "new found" strength will need to write about this

right now i am cocooned in this guilt
drowning in this bed, hiding from the globe
spinning in my own bowl of salt and water
a fish kidnapped from the sea

they tap at the glass, the windows to my soul
like some experiment, studying
wondering if i'll swim back to a place where i've never belonged
the island of you
that place was a deserted land
deserted cause you had no heart
and my love was housed in the middle of
"no where"
at the corner of dead and end
between rock and hard place
my hands were too feeble then

to justify my side

but i returned on behalf of my broken heart to pray my deliverance
and to tell you how badly you minced my internal centerpiece
you alone are a recipe for disaster
i no longer have an appetite for you
no desire for seconds

Heart*brake*

everybody's
got two hearts
as halves
most people acknowledge one
when their heart*breaks*
never admitting
the heart*brakes*

stops dead in its tracks
and maybe the person
we thought we once were
we ain't no more.

that righteous path
we thought we could skip along
is too narrow and
we don't want to skip
 no more.

see
everybody's
got two hearts
one splits
in two
halves

one beats
and its voice comes as a whisper
and says
i am hurting
the other screaming
eff it, to hell with it all
yesterday
introduced me
to heartbreak

today,
my heart*brakes*
because all that my one big heart could before
it can no longer take

At Odds

if i could wipe the slate clear
and make my heart clear
and show you my intentions
were not what they now appear;
i would.

unfortunately,
our lives are dirty
from the dirt we thrown
on each others name
and i just wish when we gazed into
the eyes of each other
it wasn't fixated on the stains

washed them away
in blood and labor
washed them away
in sweat and tears
in the love we made
in the tears that we shed

imperfect me
imperfect you
never liking what we see but knowing its the most
beautiful sight to see
you and me
i can not find any better way to spell out
how much i care for you.

i hate when you hurt
but i hate when you hurt me
and i hate that i could ever see you
standing apart from me

i just want to be your friend again
when all the romance dies and the rooms we sleep in
are down the hall
i just want to be your friend

Bind Up The Bitterness

bind up the bitterness God and help me pray
help me pray

the words that once were in me
escape me today
so help me pray
please help me pray

i have been wronged
keep my hands tightly clasped in prayer
clean of blood
keep my knees buckled to the ground
as these tears flood

every spore within me craves vengeance
i am starving to avenge my empty heart
and feast on the fullness of the penalty of their crime.

justify the sincerity of this heart of mine

and please
bind up the bitterness God and help me pray
help me pray

Delusions

its has never been documented
that the creature of the sea desired the air of sky
as they were never designed there to survive

nor has the sun been able to take
the cool of the moon
without being accompanied by light
as one defines the day
the other - night

i've never known the flowers to return to the pod
nor the butterfly to its cocoon
the piano owns its keys,
scales and octaves

the guitar resonates richly in the belly of its own wooden chamber
the violin moans bittersweet
like a woman that's been forced to abandon her lover
still remembering his caress
and whimpers through the strum of the bow
and the world has always known it so

just as one can not function as the other
neither can it be enticed by the other's vice

simply put
you are best being you
and i will always remain who God created me to be
sans the accusations of your delusions
of jealousy towards you
from me

Displaced

like a bird
forced to live in the sea
they say its wrong
for keeping your head above the salty waters
but you know you were born to fly
they tell you that you're wicked
for being able to take flight.
but you were created different
to soar
like an eagle
not to squabble with pigeons
so what gives them right to throw crumbs at your feet?

Do We Fold

life has a way of making you live it
even if you want to fight it
coax you into submission
makes you press on or it presses on you

none of us want to die but we all pray
pray to be released from the hold
one so strong it becomes a closer companion than any other
touches your heart -
aches you to the pits of your gut
life makes us feel stuck in a rut

wouldn't it be nice, if everything we drown in --- we could surface above
always needing a breath of fresh air
we hunt like wolves for the feeling of liberation, and freedom --- and elements of freedom

they say laughter is free
but it cost so much to risk investing in things that truly make us happy
like love
or like pursuing a dream
or giving it all up for what's "right"

now a days though
its like happiness and being right ain't neighbors
not even cousins:
nothing relative
we only do as they say we should feel --- by any means necessary

what does it mean to be set free?
what does it mean to be happy?

they say its a choice

but how can we choose poverty to be out of with this salary cap above us
or the deformity of our minds that shape us?
and everything with everyone
and every teaching looking
to mold us...this way and that way...

life is spinning us in circles
its spinning us in circles
like a carousel
and there are smiling faces but no one is moving
forward...just around...and a'round...

and life teases us with the gold ring that we reach for -
our arms are never long enough
to just grasp on to it.
and if we're lucky
...if we are lucky that carousel is double poled
and we can hold hands
with the kid beside us as we spin around... and a'round.
dizzy as hell
makes the emesis we vomit from the experiences of life seem
not as bad
when we share the bucket

but life gon' make you live it, alone or bonded.
and its cruelty has a tendency to rip us apart from those closest
press on cause time is pressure
and is waiting for no one to get comfortable beneath it.

Growing Pains

it is for the best that my heart has been broken
eventually my heart would have outgrown him
since this body of love is devalued to nothing but broken bones

i can

s t r e t c h

the pieces apart
so that the fractures can heal
into a wider
whole capacity of a heart
for a greater and deeper love to fill

I Can't Come Home (Part 1)

i can't come home
that house is made of glass
you tried to sway my stance
professed that 'home is where the heart is'
like that should serve as a reminder to me,
to what you could never remember
when you strayed out there.
but your heart is made of stone
and you throw your heart where ever your crotch is
and that is why the paper thin walls of this illusion have crumbled,
the roof and the bricks have shattered from the impact when you

HIT THAT

there are broken pieces every where
especially in the places that i thought we were solid
so i can't cross the threshold of the doorway anymore

it'll only make the sole of my soul bleed
and i don't need no bleeding soles on this narrow path

no, i don't need no bleeding soul on this journey

I Can't Come Home (Part 2)

you never miss a good thing until its gone.
yo' bills is all paid up, but yo' water is running dry.
how you supposed to love?
how you supposed to love?
how you supposed to love a woman when your heart so hateful inside?

you may be a bread winner
but i can't be no sinner man's significant other.
especially since i won't significant enough to keep your love exclusive from the others.
how you supposed to love?
how you supposed to love?
how you supposed to love woman when your heart so hateful inside?

your heart so hateful, your tongue *unsober*
and the answer at the bottom of your liquor container
never offers a solution to your problem.
a gambling man, drinking for the winning drop,
like each swallow is a lotto ticket.
chances are you'll never get it,
the only one in million you possessed was the woman you betrayed
and you will see...
and you will see the truth when you never again see me.

i can't come home.
cause you got to learn to lose it all, to learn how to gain it all.
or else
how you supposed to love?
how you supposed to love?
how you supposed to love a woman?

I Don't Mind

i don't mind
peeling off these layers
exposing the brown skin that
i will always be dressed in
so long as a heart is inside of me
beating

i know that my undressing
is nothing like watching the sunrise for you
but there is me
but i don't phase you
because it is me
me that you can have and conquer
like the day you wake up to seize
you think it's all for you
to build or destroy
any way
you please

you've watched this
millions of times
a new body a different curve
some ripened flesh, some skin to bones
some light
other's dark, dark as me
i know that you have run out of fingers and toes
to add up and count on
or add ribbons to remind you
"do not break this one's heart because..."

but its a radical exhilaration
you want
and every new high unlike the last
its the adventures you've had
the ones that you exploded with satisfaction in side of
you don't have to share this with anyone
all the fascinations
no you don't have to share it
unlike with love
you have to share love

because love is giving and love is kind
and hell
you've always been selfish
i know you love this
but that is it...
no one to love just the nature of this game

and i am just trying to forget something like that
that i ain't even obligated to remember
it wasn't my decision
but its stuck to my conscious
as that is your past
and its catapulting into my present
and maybe you will walk pass me
on your journey in life
and leave me in the future
and i know this
deep down i do
i can not really say why
i don't mind being another piece of wild game
you hunt and one that you will probably
consider a mantle piece over your fireplace
while you make love to some other woman
on a bear skin rug

the echo of a ton of tear drops in an empty room
falling on to the floor
ain't nothing you never heard before
has been something that you have more than
grown accustomed to
i know mine are no never mind
to you

and when did it get this way
me not giving a damn about me
but giving a damn about you
and since you too don't give a damn about me
i just want to give a damn about all you give a damn about
which is yourself
so i care about you
and i stopped caring about me

no one told me to stand here
like i am damaged goods
that you can get for half
the effort and investment
but i made it okay
to get something
out of nothing
or would it be better to say
turn something into
nothing
and i don't mind
i don't mind it being that way

I Need Your Body Heat

today
while the day is hot my heart feels cold.
i can't get warm.
last night,
felt i reached the pinnacle and reached for the pinnacle.
wished back the cherry from my coke.
chasing my liquors with coke
wishing it were coke
you were my coke - my drug
and you should have never been given my cherry.
but in both cases, for the drink; for the drug
for you
i needed something strong to stop the hurt.
i scribbled on the tablet of my heart in non legible script all the words i can not say
because i don't think you'd understand
that's why i've discontinued talking

and i can't stand that.

feeling so undeniably close to you and i can't touch you
not even as a writer with my words
that which sets me free, you say, are as barriers between us
i want to share my hurt without hurting you

or the weights of the wait of a change within me.
or without giving you the sense that
you owe me.
you owe me nothing
though you've left me
feels like i am in debt to you
though
it is more than likely
the other way around
some say...

some don't understand that you
just being here
you've given me so much then what i had before

i can say i was cared for
without being greedy
even if it ain't the way i want it
i should just be grateful like i was scolded to be
as a child and
i'm torn between the gratitude of "thank you's"
and the neediness of "don't go"
i want you to be happy with me.

and i know i don't always smile
but please know i am happy.
you make me happy
i think.

i want to share with you the smile programmed on my face as a young girl.
whether that smile was blissful ignorance, or joy or obliviousness..
there in my innocent foolishness with a childlike faith is how i want to love you.
it was a grin by default, a god-given right!   right?

that's gone now and it wasn't my fault.
i have nightmares of your love lost and i
a murder victim and it kills me to imagine
a chalk outline around me that you can't cross into
and i can't get out of
like love is life
and life was taken to a place
where love is dead to me.
and i won't believe that, no
not for a second.

the only thing i want to give you
is the joy life didn't wield for either of us
a sword against the sorrow
a secluded haven from the rain
unhappy or joyous
maybe i can be more than a lover and teach you
how to love
like i love
no one never showed you
i want you to share every moment with me
from embarrassment to endearment

and its not that you ain't my remedy i just get sick with worry.
never wanting my supply to run low or out
on me
when i need it,
and finally i'll admit and i know that i need you
i need you.
i could blame my daddy but
i know i made it so i need you always
but let's tackle
today

while the day runs hot,
and i feel so cold.
in the musk of the day and the dusk of midnight

don't be as the ice cube
boxing yourself in the cold
i am polite when i ask and include
a please
make me warm
i really need your body heat

In The Rain (a poem for Malika, because you loved the words, & because I love you)

who am i lying to?
baby my heart is broken
if it was glass it'd be scattered
why you think i'm cutting up these expressions in my face and such?
damn,
i feel betrayed
because
i've been betrayed.
telling everyone you was a good man...
... you really weren't a good man.
you pretended so well...
and i still see the good in you ...
for being that talented actor.
but even this unconditional love
always willing to extend a hand
can't lend one
can't lend two
can't applaud you for this performance...
you were smiling at me and i was crying back
as if our actions were the monolog you always scripted...
we was saying separate things.
and the scene was a massacre...
was it that way the whole time?
blood on the walls...
and blood on the floor...and blood every where
i didn't feel you stabbing me in the back...
my nerves went numb
from the impact; a hypovolemic shock
my
love never prejudice; or me so prejudice
to the shade of your dark heart.
i toss in my sheets
on the few nights i catch sleep
write it all down for sport,
can't keep it all balled up...
so i'm throwing the questions at you
hoping that even if you couldn't answer "why"
do you even feel bad for the things you do?
tell me i at least loved a man with a conscious

tell me that the things you did was painful to us both.
i never been so shamed in my flesh...
crushed in my spirit - screaming the injustice at the top of my lungs
nobody hears it.
out here - wandering heart
hoping i don't scare them off with the tears stains that i wish would
hurry up and dry on my face.
so my mask is "aloof", like i could care less...
never liked wearing these things - i'm so honest...
but i honestly can't stand them all in my business...
or in matters of my heart
that are already too hoarded with these garbage realities.
guess i'm like any other compulsive nut
and would rather this than feel empty...
cause now i got something to hold onto...
and at least its real, not pretend: like your love.
i hurt for real

Jesus & Judas

cramped in
an air tight world and left for dead in a place
without oxygen

winter is here
on the place you've asked me to lean
is where i can feel the cold frost on your shoulders
the warmth of the tears have kept me from freezing to death;
thank God i am still alive

kept my heart guarded from you
and your cruelty has activated a mechanism called survival
for this,
i thank you.
i watch you parade in the warmth of the sun
the one you've tried to shadow from my very own face

the irony of it all
for you to want everything you never wanted me to have
the stupidity of it all
to provoke me to anger with something that brought me joy
seeing the joys in life open up for you

enemy friend,
i've always seen the beauty in your masquerading
hoping one day to see a more beautiful face
sans the hideous heart you possess
you betray me with the kiss of your words
the falsification of your identity
you will perform the way you know best
my snake, you will slither...

once, so, beautiful to watch
but you are who you are
and you who you are
is who you are
venomous, scandalous, treacherous

Kitty Kat

always shooing my cat off
though she ain't nothing similar to
a needy lap dog that stay plastered to your face

always chasing my cat away
she only lingers when she purrs and needs
a soft stroke

don't be so mean to her
don't abhor the debutante gliding cross the floor
don't despise her when she reaches and stretches length wise
towards the Cape Verdean Coast
and her backsides towards the Silicon Valleys of California
she need some heat
she's tugging for attention
cause her sweet grass can't quiet her to a humble yearning

she's just bearing against your ankles for you to lift her to your lap
don't neglect her femininity
stroke when she purrs
don't neglect my cat

Lost & Found

find
myself,
never seeking to...
but find myself...
thinking of...
you.

and you don't deserve the energy it takes
to put thought to
you.

humans,
we are creatures of habit...
and i suppose
its to be understood...
that since i was here for so long...
behind
putting all of you ahead of
me
i would be lost

but i can play catch up
and real quick

i don't need you

i don't want you

but still,
find
myself,
never seeking to...
but find myself...
thinking of...
you

i got to get lost in
some place else...

thought i could live out side of my heart
where you left me
at the bottom;
with you

where you once
lived.

i kept you tucked there...
at the bottom of my heart...

but you seem to have surfaced...
floated to a top
of the waves of emotions

hope always does find a way
to float
and only to remind me

i was in love with
you
before

and then
the pain finds a way
to drown the hope again

reminds me...
i was in love with
a façade...
and the reality is
you are
a
beautiful
monster.

and i can't be there
lowered, lesser and
under
the bed
of all your extra lovers

i think i'm good with out
the tears,
the lies,
the insecurities,
the worries,
the demons;

basically all you are.

i like me more
without you.

Love Essential, Malnutrition

she ain't got no one to remember
when the old love songs play on the radio

the bass thumps harder, against the speaker
harder then the muscle in her chest
cause she ain't got nobody to reminisce

no frame of reference to latch on to
got no love to miss.
all proved false when tested
with fire.
another woman thinks on him;
he thinks on his former, her...
...and the other she had once, thinks on her, no longer

so now she,
she got no one to remember
when the old love songs play on the radio

'don't i deserve this feeling too?
...i deserve that feeling too... '
she feels.

wants to open up and speak...
wants to be as pretty as the beauty of his old memories of a former her
wants to be as perfect in his eyes as his old feelings of a former her...
the messes and all
wants him to see her with those blind eyes

she wants to hide -
she will never be as beautiful as the former love he once knew
she wants to rip herself apart and rebuild herself to be the love he wants to know

ain't no song in rotation
no old love song to play for her to remember
no love from the past...
cause she left it all there where they left her

she got no love to remember, don't nobody remember her

no one to back track and declare her the catch...
he let slip through his fingers...
no second chance
no one to desire her with every fiber...
...and she craves in turn the same hunger

don't nobody miss her, need her, want her...that way...
don't nobody got a old love song on replay
she got no one to remember - no one remembers her.

'don't i deserve this feeling?' she ponders
'...i deserve this feeling...'
she feels.

Lust

it is with absolute certainty, that if our eyes were our mouths
people would be easier to digest as a whole,
and maybe we would not be so stuffed with greed
and the gluttony of wanting

maybe we could taste it all in one glance, one helping

longing must probably be imprisoned in our sights,
pleasing to our appetite;
wondering if without the initial vision of our desire,
would it be out of mind

or maybe the over indulgence of one desire
sparks us to crave something
different, a new desire:
a new "dope"

or maybe the detrimental effects of abusing one substance
causes us to want another drug

maybe what pacified us was a gateway drug
or maybe the lack of moderation of a good thing gives us a desire for
what is impure

i could be wrong
i have been before
i more than likely will be again
i just have these thoughts

and i just have this state of being that i identify with a slang word: horny
excuse my vulgarity
i should judge all of them
and these thoughts are probably bad
they are dirty
as wicked as the ones that i have of you as i lay in this bed alone
heart cold and crotch hot

needing something new, something off limits
i know you are the fruit i should resist

you are like anything that is depleted from what my stomach craves
and thinking that without a morsel of it, it would make a head ache
you make my head pound.
i want to devour you.
i want you, in all of your glory, in all of my selfishness.
i want every fold, every crevice, every silk woven touch of your internal fluid.
every soft patch and fullness of your skin.
i want your fingers in the corner of my mouth,
i want the heat of our closeness
like my brain needs the dosage
of oxygen that fresh air supplies.
i could probably never love you the way you deserved to be loved.
i am choosing not to love you
where would be the fun in forever if i did?
but i will lust you from sun up to sun down.
i will lust you forever
i will want you for always.
because at least than if i touched you,
if i knew your body for myself
my thirst would be quenched,
and the capacity of what you offer
would be, unlike love,
measurable.

Maybe I Was A Fool

maybe i was a fool but i did
fall in love with you
yes i did.

how could we have been so close to God
our hearts bowing before each other;
and walk back into the hells of this Earth?

you knew it was something like Heaven when we were together
and your skin needed not be light for me to see the light
you just glowed
your smile, the embrace

maybe i am a fool but i did
fall in love with you.
yes i did.

the carving of your dimples
like a Greek statue, my Eros
i, Aphrodite
willing that if your restless leg syndrome desired to roam
i would come to Rome
and be your Venus, Cupid
....the sweetest of your frame
the vulnerability in your voice as you called upon
Jesus' name.

holla

but demons , even,
study quietly, the word
- to attempt to disprove God's every action
and love intention.

and the only difference in our knowledge
is our intentions
once we gained the power.

why would you opt to play QB for that team?
did he promise you the kingdoms and palaces of this Earth;

or for the wisdom and skill of an archeologist and the strong tools
to be handled in your mouth
through your teeth
in the form of words and a tongue
to clench the hard stones diamonds in the erect nipples of another woman's breast?

and a warm mouth for your soft bristle words
to brush away the dust of concern
on top of the grave another man buried her under
while her corpse is yet rising?
sort of how you've done me
as i was returning to life.

maybe i was a fool but i did
fall in love with you
yes i did.

Not Mine

why
am i laying besides you
in your arms?

in your bed
one that doesn't belong to me anymore

...arms that she wrongfully claimed.
a heart that's mine and dwells in you...
one you always refused me

and whose right?
and whose wrong?

figured
maybe if i returned
just for a little while
i could steal my heart back from this place
while you were preoccupied
sexing me
thought it was in one of these inanimate objects
the leather couch... the guest room, the corner nook i used to write in

but you've still got it in your hands, toying with it
i see it
and, i am still powerless, can not retrieve it
and what a fool i am to feel at home
in a former house that isn't set up for me to find any rest
not in the form of peace
nor to rest my head
nor to rest my heart
nor to rest my soul

Scripting Erasable Monogamy

i feel like i don't belong anywhere on this green earth right now
i wish i had wings
...wings to fly high above the world i live in

that high up,
i could make all the big things, small
i wish i had wings to fly closer to God and hear everything He wants to tell me
...i would listen to Him, & not them

not even myself...
emotions get loud.
i am human, with error.
i wish i could hear His voice & silence wasn't screaming so loud in my ears.

but all i have are legs, so i'll run...
and all i have are hands...
so i'll write,
write the wrongs til i right the wrongs

i hate the regrets that taught me...
...angry with the naivety that refuses to keep me
i hate the bitter truth...i want the sweet waters of lies.
that would be easier to swallow.
but poison never purged any of us -

my heart feels polluted...
wish i could clear the air.
i just want to clear the air...
until i can i'll be holding my breath
waiting to exhale.

Sucker Punch

if she were made of steel
she would be an awesome conductor
of your heat
and it would transfer to the freezing world around her
and when you kissed her and lit up her heart
the world would shine; how brightly she would radiate

and as a woman
she can do nothing but mirror
your Excellency
as she was created excellently
after God had mastered every other creation
He took his artistic hands and went beyond perfection
and there stood a woman.

if she were a lens
she would guard your eyes
and give you clarity
and insight into everything near
and far that blinded you
that is the way a woman's heart is designed to love
and process and operate.

without any uncertainty
if she were a breeze
she would circle you from head to foot
on the hottest days and send her warmest currents
through the fronts of the cold during the winter months
fighting through for you

of all the things she could be
and that you could ask her to be
and that she would transform into willingly
for you
a punching bag
has become your favorite tool

The Crushing Law of Gravity

for every action
there is an equal
and opposite reaction
naturally
when you caressed me
i came to life

you rose to the occasion
i fell head over heels
my love came down to meet you

but you rose with the sun
and moved your shine and took your light
for the rest of the flowers of the world

now i'm left in the dark with my collapsing petals
wilting over the science of love
questioning the theories
becoming an innocent bystander of its extinction

Tremors

should of heeded the warnings
when i was little girl
not to play with my shadow
only made a mockery of the light
by turning my back against it
just to idolize the illusions i could create.

but i was too fascinated with the dancing on the wall
to realize that i evoked the games to life
falling in love with the shadow of a man

...too fascinated with what was done in the dark...

and the shadows of our bodies
dancing on the walls.
i turned my back against the light.
the mockery is me.
no one can ever hold fleeting darkness
no matter how great the mass of it...
no matter how strong the imagination
and imagination
sometimes
wants to envision a fairytale, into a happily ever after.

a nightmare is a nightmare that we must suffer until we wake up.
i'm awake now
and still trembling

Untitled #0

where's my link?
why doesn't anyone know when my heart is crying?
can't you hear it shattering?
why isn't anyone rushing to figure out the clamor?

all this noise
all these pieces

i can't cry in front of them...

they'll just think me weak...
they'll tell me i'm wrong for being human

cause i always got to be Superwoman.

whose gonna come save me?
i looked in the mirror so much at her...save yourself...
but i can't right now.

no one hears me...no one knows...its all here but no one knows.

these solitary places are cold.
my finger tips are bitten.
difficult to grip this pen and sketch the letters
and paint this picture for anyone
in the form of a poem.

why can't anyone feel me?
this pain confirms it and i am...

ALONE

can't i trust anyone in this world with my weakness:

"love"

Un-Unconditional

thought it was time

but i suffer my mother's habit
of getting ahead of myself

and though i have a heart
i lack the heart
to endure the patience
that love requires
to deal with anyone
even a "once in a lifetime" you
outside of my own terms

which have yet to be defined.

Winter Has Come

all i have is you
the life i keep trying to run from
and the four walls that won't offer any distance.

every prayer that is prayed comes out in the form of a whisper
though i pray it becomes loud enough to be heard
answered, honored...

still
all i have is you

the words of a former love
the words of my very own lies
echo in my ears
that life is pain
and that every story ends in sadness
and though i've been delivered from him
from those words
that belief; seemingly a curse
i've not yet, been

so i wallow here
being shallow here
holding onto that philosophy of his
that seems truer now than it ever did
staring for an escape inside of
yellow incandescent lights, neon bright pink
trying to find the tenderness of life and living...

but reality is so harsh and wraps its self around me
like a blanket.
and this emptiness fills me
and this is the only company i know.
i've never known me so well, and i have never felt so alone.

Wise Up

wise up girl
that's the same spirit with a different face.
same familiar spirit gon' keep following you
until you get like Jesus
and use that authority and rebuke it.

say get thee hence behind.
like the old church folk say.

its the same spirit that's going to over power you and shake you,
break you down to the marrow of the bones of your soul
use its words to attempt to CRUSH you to build itself up.
because no spirit in its likeness would ever cast out its own
and you know you come in love

so why he always got to hate?

it can't be a part of you
because it is unlike you
so cast it afar from you.

yes, he's a different man,
lighter skin, longer penis
pinker lips, slender, taller frame...
but that spirit babygirl
that spirit is the same.
and it ain't with flesh and blood you
that you battle -
its the vibe
the auras
the "feelings"
that "thang" that you get when he's around
that prince you think is a prince is a principality

and in his presence

you don't quite feel as high as you did before
cause he don't give you power
but you got power to tread serpents

even in the form of him
and the stiff one between his thighs
and God had said He would make your enemies your footstool;
but he wants to treat you like a foot stool
he'll call you for tail, never putting you ahead of anything else
and the only thing you're headed for is destruction

no baby girl
that ain't the way love GOES.
black butterfly, you are no moth to no flames...
no matter how high those flames of passion are
i am told love goes like this
its patient and kind, and courageous.
and if this is too much to ask of us
that we be exalted like the queens we have to learn to carry ourselves to be
queens and royalty like that in which God made us to be -
then WAIT for the man who is brave enough to embody
God

the God that has taught HIM to love HER
...unconditionally.
the one that wants you covered up,
because he knows a diamond is covered, deep
and must be found, not obtained easily
seal off your temple, protect your worth
and wait, wait for him.
wait for the man that allows love to flow through him,
and accepts that love flows to him.

BELOVED

A Poem for Mommy

it is because of lovers that have come and lovers that have gone
that i've learned why i always found joy in your laughter
and in the short comings of myself
that i erupt with frustration when i see your faults

i will never be able to write a poem to you in the conventional way
through the tunnels of compassion and admiration
as you are an unconventional woman
and those tunnels would only find us both
in a state outside of where we currently reside
in awkwardness

i guess i've become the warrior you made us to be
with our four letter expression best done in action
this is for the sacrifice, regardless of your intentions
this is for all i hold you responsible for, sans the blame
this is for making the most of little, and doing the best you could
this is for making heat out of an oven
a bedroom out of a mattress and a kitchen floor
this is for making food from particles, a dollar out of fifteen cents
this is still with apprehension, but in reverence to your preference and existence;
with a dash of discomfort and a heap of my developed cool

this is written in the original format,
even and in the smallest script
in the loudest form, as the softest answer:
since i love you never works the same for you as an unconditional
no strings attached simple
THANK YOU

A Soft Answer

my strength may be quiet but it is strength none the less
my love may be slow to conquer but the spoils are endless
my breath may escape me
and i may lose the words i have to find to say what needs to be said
but i will always tell you the truth
and i will always come from a place of love

all the moments that we catch in the place of all we've lost
are worth far more because something new will always be found
we may become familiar
and cease to anticipate with anxiousness
every caress
we may cease to tremble with each touch
or shiver with each and every kiss
but a new level of love will be discovered
in the guarantee your love will always be with me
we can build off of this promise

i may weep
but it is only because my heart functions properly to feel
show me nothing less than what your life is destined to be
as you share your life with me

i may be pained in my soul
but only when you are apart of me as 'we' feels complete
and i lack what makes me whole when you're gone
my exterior may be hard
but i promise my heart is flesh
and just as equally bruised as yours

All Of The -*ism*'s

when i was tender; when i was kind,
when i was meek; when i was mild
when i told you
i LOVE you
just because
being in LOVE was the sole reason

when it was easier to smile
when it was easier to cry
and with no hesitation
i would lay it all down and die for you
i used to know how to love

now i've gotten over analytical
super philosophical, ultra astronomical
wishing there were no "IF's" as a theory
no "AND's" as a law
and no "BUT's" to negate any of the simple fact that
i
LOVE
you

And The Band Plays On (part 1)

either way we'll flourish in forever
or feel the exhilaration of how fickle our depiction of love is

and glory
glory be to God!

whether its heaven or hell on Earth
we'll keep breathing
even if we hardly are

the pain may feel suffocating
the pressure, crushing every thing

and glory
glory be to God!

whether rain or snow
we'll keep breathing
we'll find a way
to keep breathing

Bare Naked Love Pleasantries (*a poem for Eddie*)

i love you for being able to see me in human form
and not just in written form

i've been told, like most writers, homely and plain
i am far more charming and brave through my ink;
more reserved and not as legible on the surface

but you were wise enough to observe God's greatest oxymoron
the dichotomy of me as a whole
by never judging my cover, exploring every chapter...
you are helping to write this happy ending
to one of the greatest love stories ever told

i love you for loving a mess like me
my living habits aren't as orderly and flowery as my handwriting
and you were patient enough to wait out the incessant gnawing of my pencils
pen tops, nail tips and acrylic.

you see me beyond the stanzas, the verses, the songs, the page...
to others i am an enigma, to you, an open saga

i love you because,
even with the make up off, you believe i am gorgeous
i love you because,
even with the make up on, you see what truly makes me gorgeous

you say that its the nature of my heart
and i say that without you and your tender love,
it would have no world to survive in

El Oh Vee Ee (Love)

love
be in love with me
because
like air
you are better experienced
than explained
apart i am at your mercy
attached
i am free
yet bound by your existence.

i need you love
i need you beyond the demands of wanting you
you are the foundation on all i am built upon
in all forms of probability
in every pocket of reality
where can i find you if you aren't lost
and at times that you feel so distant?
where can i be that you aren't?

i feel you
as common as light,
in variations of gradients
in the scheme of darkness
punctured in to elevation like altitude
hallowed in the decline of the deepest canyon
shifting the phases of the moon
fueling the fire of the sun

outside of myself
on the two way street of consideration
through the eyes of another
in the acts of sincerity
in the breath of kindness
in the caress of willingness
on my knees in self sacrifice
in the embarrassment of an apologies
in the reluctance of forgiveness
that is where you are

like a frame of reference
when life is off balance
you are the reset button to a game awry
pH 0 from the bitter lemons of life
and the cavity inducing sweets of syrup
if my life were a hiccup
you come in the form of water
if pain were air pressure trapped in my ear canal
you are the yawn that frees it
you are both the disillusionment of a dream
and the realities of fantasy
where feet can be planted
you are ground they stand on
and where clouds nest atop like sparrow birds
you offer a canopy of sky
you are the expression of your creations in their entirety
praised for their individuality
and the ecosystem you provided for them to function in
no place in this world is without life to be hosted
though i have, at times, found myself
outside of my element
you sustained me

love is within all
and i need you love
where ever you can be manifested
and where ever you can share
the embrace of your presence
i need you love
to follow my footsteps
and remain latched to my ankles
in place of the shadows that try to follow
and in the form of a holy spirit
guide my steps
into the place where the sun shines at my face

where my vision is blurred
love corrects my eyes to see all that is unseen
and i need you love
not to just love me
but to be in love with me

and where you call to me
do not let silence fall to my ears
but lift up the volume of joy in my life
because i need you
i need you more than ever before
i've prayed for love
but not to be in love with you
not like this before
and i now know
that i have never known love
no
not like this before

God,
for being you;
for being above and beyond all that i am able to comprehend
and utter in the form of a prayer or poem;
for choosing to express me
in the form of life through DNA;
as a vessel with infinitely many
possibilities
thank you

Ellipsis

do i need to add the ellipsis
or is it understated that i pause before i confess
...i love you
please don't ask for an emphasis
in phrasing or stressing individual words
as formulating the idea is difficult enough

not so much of the
you
as it is not such that odd of a thing
that something God created at the prime of His artistic expression
is admired as such:

a masterpiece
and that you are.
or the entity of
I;
fearfully and wonderfully convex in the breast,
concaves at the lower extremities of the waistline and spine

but the awareness,
and the audacious presence,
the elite existence;
better yet acceptance of
love
living inside of me,
again.

it may be read from my hand script but this does not happen quite often
if you consider my fondness to rejection ratio
but i believe its so

your angel has found a way to escort you into the REM stages of my sleep
into the bottom of my heart, at fore front of my mind;
and time traveling, placed you in my forever

i'm just trying to find a way to tell you that i am never letting you go.

i just need you to find a lane to get comfortable in
as a friend, or a confidant,

a king underneath the King of kings, passionate lover;
though i would prefer you just be everything...
i will be thankful with anything.

Foolish of I

my God how many times in this life will you find me on bending knees?
how ungrateful have i been to expect a god out of a man?
he may be made in your image but i mistook that as a carbon copy
the devil masters all perversion
all things counterfeit
i fell for fools gold
and everything that glitters is not gold

there is none like you
only one like you
and that Father, my God, is you.
how unworthy of your love have i been to put faith in what you created?
loving the gift more than the gifter

how ignorant to ever think
that these bodies that bleed and break and turn to dust
could embody the capacity of your everlasting, undying love?
i cried these tears with a broken heart while breaking your heart as you rose me up
day to day with sunshine
acting like the rain was created to follow me like a black cloud
forgetting to say thank you
cursing the pain and worshipping the hurt like it had been everything...
and you were being everything to me that my blinded eyes refused to see

i may say it with these lips
but my actions were all the more reflective of someone that was just sorry
how pathetic have i been?
more pathetic than he for hurting me
i cried these tears with a loss of hope never knowing your hope was not like earthly hope
...disregarding the expectancy of a certain fruitful ending....kind of hope.

you commanded me to never cease praying
once i had...
i allowed a man to bring me to my knees, foolishly.
at least falling to my knees for you always built me up.

i ignored your promise for a future that was never promised
with a vessel that was dead end

i cursed the ground i walked with my negativity
turning my sight against this narrow path
how ungrateful have i been to never say thank you for carrying me?
how ungrateful have i been for falling victim to weakness?
there are many sins that have been performed with the influence of lust and coveting, but to place a feeling, doubt and anger ahead of you
i've idolized and worshipped like foreign gods.
and i see it now.
my surviving the blows, the potential diseases that could have been contracted
the pregnancies, the abortions, the animosity and jealousy
from unrequited rage filled women
the death from the accidents as wake up calls
you tried to tell me
all the odds
and all i can say is Abba, heavenly Father, forgive me.

pity my simplicity
you loved me more than i loved me
yet still you ordered my steps
i realize my hard head suffered me, to come to thee.
and there is no better place to be.

Never A 365 for Each Tear

his lips parted
hissed
her skilled in knowing
when a sincere apology
was a sincere apology
when a
'please forgive me, I've done a bad thing
to a good woman'
was sincere

this was not one of those cases
and out of habit, and sense
she was mindful to take his body of words
and drop a grain of salt on them
and name each one
and inscribe those names with a bullet
incase feelings wanted to become
like Lazarus and rise up again
lie
lies
and *more lies*
is what she called them.
and so it was.

he spoke of the sleepless nights
haunted halls,
new women he knew but did not know
how he was *still restless on the hunt for some*
strange
but that its getting old and he thinks he changed
or would for the right woman
translated, she knew he meant
the right fool or desperate circumstance
to make him buckle his knees
and play a new role for the sake of sympathy
or when the times got tight
he could see the light

she parted her lips, matter of factly-grin and replies

is that right?
a silence falls that he dribbles his, *"...yeahs"*
in between and wipes his chin, reaches for his pride
lowers his guard from across his chest
rests it across his arms and extends it towards her
...a game to him, on the rebound and coming
to retrieve a play after his last of many fouls.
she knew that though he had attempted to devalue her to silver once
she was now platinum, and she was now gold
and the same, as he spoke, he found the same mineral
buried in her silence

he, in amazement of her maturity, deliverance
belittling of his presence, began to profess to her
his undying
unknowing
couldn't run away from
love for her
poured his entire heart in

and she, prepped with needle in hand
a lethal injection, interjects
his heart felt confession
admitting, that though *the nights were cold*
The days long
Separation stabs, strong
She *would rather take her chances in the uncertainties of life*
Than to be his familiar fool, dunce of a wife
And *that if God granted* her *one day plus the time*
She *shed for* him *in tears*
She wouldn't take him back in a million years

Guilty (I Am Looking At You)

i am guilty of rushing and not taking the time to slip into the imprints of the tiny soft wrinkles and fingers of my own hand.

i am guilty of not coating my nail lacquer correctly and letting the polish chip and biting them frantically, and picking at my cuticles.

i am guilty of damaging my hair with heated ceramic plates and leaving my contact lenses in for days at a time.

admittedly,
encouraging my gene to remain with limited visibility.

i don't always floss and i poke at my gums with a toothpick when all my cuticles are gone.

i'm chronically obsessed with order, so long as it pertains to anything internal.

my memories are grouped with intensity of emotion, but i always seem to remember the laughter before and after the pain.

i am subject to random out burst of laughter.

no external stimulants needed to provoke this.

i dig in my left ear religiously but act like i can't hear no body.

my right hand never knows what my left hand is doing, but some how i can always mediate between the two that they meet to pray.

i am a woman of habit who is probably easy to love, but push so hard to be easily understood that most just find my standards difficult to comprehend.

i curl my hands into balls, and into my pocket and rarely ornament the tool that has given me the most satisfaction - on page and in my panties.

and
i am ashamed that i see so much greatness in others that to balance the realism i find the negative in myself.

you see

i am guilty for squealing in my sleep because though no more swine will touch mine, i can't forget i enjoyed the taste of bacon.

and there is no room under my sagged breast to tuck the waistline of my size 8 "skinny" jeans over my size 10 gut.

and i am guilty of rushing and not taking the time to slip into the imprints of the tiny soft wrinkles and fingers of my own hand.

one of these days
i will venture into the canyons of my tit gourds
hallow my joined palms and drink the waters in the shallow of my belly button,
grab a surf board,
and ride the torrent hip waves of my stretch marks
to the other ends of the world
to caress and embrace
my beautiful ass

Happily Ever After

in rare cases, that are not rare
just not as circulated by mouth as other
fairytales involving a prince often are

happily ever after does not always include a
14 karat platinum, white gold, solid gold, rose gold or yellow gold band
with a blood, or pure diamond
elongated as an emerald, mirrored in its arrangements as an asscher,
kaleidoscoped in its center like a marquise,
mounted on its throne like a princess or portioned out and sliced
from the sky into a pretty square.

in rare cases it does not need a pure white mermaid dress
with the freight of a train chasing behind it
nor is it an aisle of orchids and tulips
and dainty love sick maidens as maids
to a bride
thirsting for the groomsmen
waiting on their turn to hitch

it isn't a man rescuing a damsel in distress.

in rare cases, not that rare
just not as circulated by mouth like other fairytales

a princess recognizes that her Father
Jehovah
is a King
and rightfully claims her throne
on the validation of the Prince of Peace
interceding for her life, through His death,
by way of her heavenly Father, alone;
and she realizes, she is to die for.

in rare cases,
not that rare,
just not as socially exalted as finding a man
and "putting a ring on it" is...
a woman will stand before a mirror
and learn to smile at her imperfections and wash away the impurities

and learn to oil her face and not bury her natural beauty with
maybelline, but should she decide to don her palate with colors
will do so tastefully
because she likes it that way.

in rare cases, not that rare
just not as smiled upon as announcing of an engagement
a woman will make a commitment to aspire for more.

cloth her self in better garments and choose to be
patient with herself and take the time
to make time to be good to herself
and she will cast down every vain and evil thought
that tears her apart
and rebuke the hateful things her past whispers.
as evil things can tend to want to be more powerful than
the promise her Father made...
as she knows that she is fearfully and wonderfully made.

in rare cases, not that rare
just not as influenced as finding a husband is or
as forced or influenced upon little girls and
negatively reinforced to grown women;
a woman will remember the restlessness of her childhood
and remember the scratching of destiny at her heart.
she will recall to memory the desire to conquer and conquest and
discover the varieties of culture, the climate of expressions
and the temperature of the seasons within her life.
and she will be brave and she will say in her heart and she will know
i am enough.

i am that i am
enough.
like my Father, like my God.

since Adam's ribs formed a whole she
than what can be duplicated from the very tiny particle of me?
like the tips of my fingers to a pen...
what can i create with the gentle touch of my hands?
the opening of my lips and the well of words from my mouth
the electromagnetic fields of my brain,
the pounding of my heart?

if i, woman, came from the rib of a man...
what creation can spring from me?

these are the things she will think when she knows she is enough
and the race she runs is no longer weighed down
by the expectations of man,
the envy of false friends,
the self inflicted insecurities of her mind and
the encumbrances of her sins
when she believes in herself

a complete, wholeness, of her
made in the image of an infinite God
with innumerable probabilities and possibilities.
and once she finds she is happily comfortable in her own skin...
anything that follows after,
at any time, in any way thereafter
is the true definition of a happily ever after.

Now & Then

without the exhaust of a lengthy explanation
the difference between then and now is
desperation / necessity
need / want
option / priority
compensation / complementation

just as a tooth is not genuinely whole
once its rotted, gutted, filled
with some artificial hard substance
it could have never been full genuine love
as the benefits were only sought to make up for
the deterioration of a rotting heart
from internal decay

Him

if you only knew
how much of a thief i've become
stealing glimpses of the bronze of your skin
the arch and the dip of your brow
the curve in your lips
the cashmere felt of your kiss;
i've never had any intent to return to you
any part of you.
i was always taught the universe was bigger than us all
but i'm leaning into your arms like it were the wind wrapping me in the breeze
and i find the warmth of the season in the rays of your presence.
my hunger for you has become animalistic,
every part of me aching almost howling for the magnetic energies you bring to me at night
i am satisfied with the galaxy you have flown me through
on our trips to the moon
right there where you make love to me.
say you love me
say you love me
and my nights will rise to day
and the rain will cease to fall
and the cold will dissipate

Karma

one can come
dragging in
apologies that smell like
dead rodents
performing the way they used to
naturally and eloquently scripted
in deception
unknowing that an apology
unknowing that forgiveness
will not alter
will not reverse
anything that was offset in the universe
by the works of their very own hands
and the meditation of an unchanged heart

with centripetal force
a circular motion
the movement of karma spins around
and repays
all that is vested
and the outcome
makes the intent evident

karma. karma. karma.
it always comes back
three times as hard
                    my heart has learned to forgive
                                        and i am indifferent to its dealings with you

unknowing that greed
unknowing that harm of others for personal gain
does not
will not
can not alter or change
what was offset in the universe

with centripetal force
a circular motion
the movement of karma spins around

and repays
all that is vested
and the outcome
makes the intent evident

karma. karma. karma.
it always comes back
three times as hard
my heart has learned to forgive
and i am indifferent to its dealings with you

Love U 2 Pieces

love dissolves hate
and love happens to be what made me
and all that i am made of
is that why you so frivolously
crumbled around me?
ran cowardly?
where love is,
hate can not,
hate will not survive in the atmosphere with its stench of envy.
s'll good.
i will still LOVE you
all to pieces.

Scratching The Surface

look in the mirror
and tell me who you see.
someone powerful: that powerful woman is me.

beat of your own drum,
patterned to a simple melody -
the tempo ticking in my mind
keep reminding myself
i can do and be anything: i am strong enough
to conquer anything this time.

i hear the laughter -
but truth always prevails, rises to claim her own.
holding me down; even while i am down on my own.
look in the mirror and tell me who you love
someone incredible: that incredible woman is me.

fresh as a cool breeze during a humid summer
dainty daisies suffocate before you
other flowers will wither beside you, but not you
it will not come near your dwelling

look in the mirror and tell me whose arrived.
someone becoming of herself
ready to come alive

that woman of intrigue
i never thought i would meet you
but that wonderful woman
finally
that wonderful woman is me

Something Else

no deception would ever become appealing
if it, first, was not a part of our appetite
if we do not first lie to ourselves
how would we crave being lied to?

mirror, like a mirror,
every relationship, person reflecting and refracting
all that is within and manifesting all that we are.
what is it that makes it seem so fulfilling
disgusting toxic things, entertaining toxic people

it is human nature to materialize all that we envision
all that we focus our energies on in our mind
so we take the abusive talk
and we honor the disloyal friend
and we hold on with fear
the agents of manipulation that we know will one day hurt us
because we are afraid to be alone
because we are afraid to lose God if we let go
we act like we have no ties to God
like people are our saviors

something else
i know its something else
and it ain't the love that i would like to call it.
we idolize people in hopes that our admiration
will act as some form of righteousness
and credit of our reference of holiness

something else
i know its something else
the faith that drives out fear
just won't work if we don't choose it
over the fear
or if we don't realize that even that
faith is what we need
to love ourselves
cause lord knows it ain't easy

what belief can anyone give us

to see the best in ourselves?
what can be said or done to make us believe we deserve
the good that is in store for us
if we always focus on what we lack?
all these "things" we search for to fill up our voids
just to avoid facing the fact that
"i am enough"

The First Time I Made Love

didn't want to even bother to shower
all the strength leapt from my body
and all this love i couldn't contain
it broke free from my heart
i couldn't hold it anymore

when my love escaped
it left in its wake
throbbing rib cages, barely clenching to the hinges
blowing in the gust of gale force winds
winds channeled through air dried lips
lips like funnels for two exhaling lungs
panting, inhaling
pumping for oxygen to keep the fire going

like coal in my blood stream;
my heart was a freight train, speeding
speeding like a freight train was my heart

it was the kind of love that after making
lingered
drunk and on an open tab
too intoxicated to stomach anymore
of a refill

we were one
but individually
two lovers with lazy lips
intense tenderness
tongue lapping tongue like two thirsty dogs
mid summer for pond water
thirsty for love that had dried in our wells

hand to face caressing the boarders
like a perfect framed picture
of a memory to cherish and always remember

my lover's fingertips becomes ten individual hands -
massaging the roots... the strands
each individual, kinky, root...mattered

it was the kind of love that after making
the only coarse he'd been concerned with
was the course he'd taken to arrive at the destination of
"loving me"
the right woman
right up my ally

we laid there
funky scent smelling like pure desire
and sweet forbidden fruit;
all stirred up in an aroma
beat into a coma with a contact high.
only smelled good to the users

it was the kind of love that after making
my lover read my soul
through the braille of goose bumps
rising at his touch

it was like that
where the orgasm ran a relay of sprints
from the cuticles of my toes
to the chattering of my wisdom teeth
then collapsed in the glory of his instrument
exploded with a song

all i could offer was a chime
and in i came resonating in unison
a cry outward
the harmonies of our love in concert
the symphony of love making
replayed on repeat in the play list of my mind
a tune that has become a favorite melody
in the soundtrack of our lives

The Issue is You

one day
there will be no one to point
an index finger at
and say the turn is yours
in the blame game

one day
there will come a time
when your thoughts
circumstances, situations
all have a mutual contact
and they will introduce you to
that individual
that you have tried to ignore
and remove from the equation

one day
running from the problem
will no longer be an option
and you will find
you've been the rodent
in a spinning wheel
moving no where
but in circles

one day
when you are tired
of lending your power
to other factors
outside your person;
you will come to understand
accept and comprehend
the issue is you

I Do Adore (for my Sisters & my Girls)

i do adore
adore you i do
ask of me anything
and my all i'll give to you

if what i have read was true
that every relationship in our lives
are direct reflections of who we are
i must stop to stare
can't help but glare
when i look in the mirror
when i look at you
i see : beautiful
without you
my validation in life has no petition
but my own breath
with you i can take on the world
with you my prayers have a muse
my silence a purpose
my madness a method
we are stars that shine bright,
never afraid to share the vast sky
cause we know God has spread a wide blanket
called the universe
for us to take claims of our individual galaxies
everything i treasure
i find within your acts of kindness, compassion
often finding pieces of my heart buried in the gemstones of wisdom that you possess
i share in your happiness like a victory for the team
and fight the battles by your side as your right hand
you cover the stains of blood on my hands like a sheath to an iron dagger
and correcting me just the same
my blade remains sharpened
never a cruel word has left your lips
never a lie or deceit
never betrayal or insecurity
never manipulation or ill intent
i am one hundred percent for you
as you are one hundred percent for me

so its you

you i do adore
adore you, i do
ask of me anything
and my all i'll give to you

There is More

there is so much more beyond this
so much more than someone's flesh and bones
a sack of skin to stuff what took nine months to develop
and come to be an entire life
inside of.

there would not be enough room
for all this love and appreciation to fill

so many other objects to reflect an image
not just within the eyes of a human
there are many waters of distant lands
that engulf shores filled with tropical things
coral reefs, salted and fresh waters
made just for dreamers and go-getters like me to see

and not only to be seen with my eyes
but there are audible waves these sounds in the form of drums
flamingos and airy flutes, warm brass bells and whistles
chimes and horns
colors and gradients
and elements in the form of fire
symphonies and scores alike that want to compose,
find the key signature, orchestrate
harmonize, dissent against,
paint and splash their connotation of
my individuality on this canvas we call life

and what an insult it would be to minimize the potential
of the portion
of a great divine Being flowing within me
and cram it into the point of view of one species:
mankind
especially when the probabilities of any given experience are endless
and man is so finite
but, God, so infinite
and all He wants to do in His abundance is use Us

Au Natural

you live in a world
where you are born loved from the top of your silky head of hair
to the soles of your moon walking feet
and i've been placed in a world
where the qualifications to being loved
begins at the texture of my nappy headed roots and usually stop there
for most
its too tough a coarse to get past

i've been placed in a world
where i been trained since youth to press
and straighten
and relax
what comes natural to me

psychologically, i was born in the "wrong"
so i been told to get "right"
make it look more
Indonesian
Korean
Hawaiian
Indian
white
stressing me out about what's kinky, curly, knotty
see in my world, most of my own men frown upon *au natural*
its more "ugh, (she's) natural",
and its more likely he will choose someone that does not look
anything like me.
because i have been told i am not a symbol of beauty.
and who wants to live in exile?
it is why we behave like sheep
and it is easy to conform with our wool sheep hair,
and just get what ain't broken "fixed".
even want to save our kids
from the natural deficit that these enhancements cause.
so we burn our scalps to find a *good* man,
or more like a man with "GOOD"
smooth baby making hair
so our little girls don't go through
what mommy went through during mating season

with our weaves extra expensive quick fix, cheap synthetic and human hair, shedding.
we want her to be
"PRETTY"
and maybe while we conceive,
we can pretend in the heat of the moment
"he truly loves me...for all of me - and the straight extension he sees"
see i can't speak for every sista'
i am one pen in one woman's hand attached to one body with one voice
i don't know every "correct" word
that i'm allowed to use for the "afro centric"
or the "revolutionaries"
cause revolutionary for me is facing the ugliest parts of me and fighting these demons
i'm too domesticated
to knock it out the way "ghetto fabulous" ones want it done,
too raw for the religious ones - too uneasy to speak for the relaxed,
too modest in my material collection for the high fashioned,
and too mad in my methods to be the voice of the free- spirited,
too down to earth for the homely ones
so i'll just say it the way my heart feels it:
baby,
it'll probably never be down my back,
and you got to be okay with that.

What The World Needs Now

there are bombs exploding in Boston
and innocent brown faces being suspected
because their parents named them
Rashid and Reham
and grown white men
can kill young black boys in "safe" neighborhoods
all for carrying a cellular device and a pack of skittles
and that is a crime
being innocent and having the face of what is looked upon as a common criminal
and it is a clear indication of prejudice that gets covered up by the media just like the millions of cases with missing black victims
my black and brown sons being imprisoned
or missing ain't that big of a deal to the rest of the world because
dark is easier to cover underneath the dirt

this isn't a poem about racism though
that isn't my intention

i just want to address a concern i have for my unborn child
and your child too, despite the shade of the reader
because black or yellow, or green, or white
they would be lucky to make it into the fifth grade alive
physically or mentally
or out of their mother's wombs

something is off spiritually; seriously

something is wrong
when i can't run my race of endurance to get my prize
without my enemies posing as friends
setting explosives to tear my limbs and legs off
and something is terribly wrong when news like that comes as no surprise
and 26 kids are murdered because someone is sick
and no one can take the time to cure it
and no one knows how
and maybe they do
but they would prefer the lumps sum of money
to be hand delivered before they deliver you from the mental hostage
and anguish they could free you from, at no cost

it cost us so much to be so greedy with our priceless knowledge
as if we have something to lose

and all any of us can say upon hearing the news
is "that's messed up"
and shake our heads and post our statuses
as if our font is making a difference in anyone's consciousness
and sip our coffee and keep living just incase our number is up next
but ultimately we living like
...it ain't nothing...
when truthfully
we are just glad we
"don't have to be bothered"
something is terribly out of whack when a background check needs to be conducted to determine the condition of my heart
because no one has access to the holy spirit anymore to discern whom and what they are dealing with anymore

no one wants to get to know anyone anymore
its not an accusation or placing it in anyone's hands
for i am just as responsible for turning a blind eye
to the hateful slurs of my African and Hispanic
and Latino and East Indian
and West Indian and Asian
and Indonesian and European
sisters and brothers
and or ignoring the insults
and hatred of anyone toward the other regardless of race,
age, creed, sex, genetic retardation or impairment
who am i to judge?

its the love of money and the love of power
and the love of pride that keeps the hate alive
and by any means we all want to be right
and i am getting to a place where i would rather be happy than right
i don't even care anymore its just that
maybe we all are damned if we do
and damned if we don't

all i know is something is wrong
when a young girl is forcing a finger down her throat
to make sure her skeletal frame defines the beauty of her figure

and disregards her muscular structure
as a factor
and when the words to express their pain isn't coming out
as easily as it does for others they vomit

others are stuffing food down their throats
to fill a space they can't reach
i am weeping for my children's children
because they are in trouble if we don't start agreeing
maybe not so much on these political issues
those haven't solved much
not that i have seen in my twenty some odd years i've been here
its so much verbal jargon no one understands it all
and everything is a loophole for lies to reign supreme over the truth
but if we can all just get over ourselves and our titles and admit
something is wrong
and there is something bigger than us all that we are trying to live without
and its LOVE.

something in me told me that the answer is in us
but the answer ain't us
and we've all got guts
but some lack the heart
and i know that God is in there
if we just let Him lead us and speak through us and to us
i don't know if we've gotten so comfortable
writing the other off and discrediting the people we don't understand
maybe we feel as if we are running out of time
and we ain't got time to figure each other out
we want to be admired and loved by "numbers" instead of respected by people
i know families and members that brush the other's behavior off
and would more than likely judge their actions by "that's just them"
and labor more to tear them apart
than to labor in prayer
as if we aren't connected with the same silver lining.

i can not judge or speak on it
if i myself were not guilty
and i can not point the finger at the failing human condition
when it comes to love
all i can do is be aware and be there
and try to change it with every interaction that i can access

my daddy taught me better than anyone else
there is no fire of anger so powerful that is can not be quenched by the grave
as there is no coming back from death
and why do we always wait for someone to die
before we bring them flowers
they can not smell it there
you can not feel the joys in the peace of forgiveness there
and there is no sincerity in the pits of hell
and i hope to never go to the grave with anyone not knowing i forgave them
because guilt is such a heavy burden to bear.

i just know something is wrong
it doesn't feel right
and that is all the indication that any of us need
and our tears and our suffering
and our pain and the destruction
does not have to serve as some pre-requisite
or requirement or rite of passage
to peace and happiness
it shouldn't take all of this madness to have an appetite for peace
is there something embedded deep within us that make us addicted to hurting?
where is the fullness in the simplicity?
why do we complicate so much and feel so poorly of ourselves?
why do we take faith in the lifeless promises of someone that hasn't found
themselves and not in the power of our very own existence?
haven't we known ourselves all of our lives
why can't we embrace even ourselves?

i get afraid sometimes that love will become extinct
and so far from the truth of what people are to know it to be
i become so afraid
that what i perceive as love is in fact
a generic off centered perception of it
influenced by my society
or my lack of resources in which it can survive

its not about being deep
but i think that something is wrong
when the medicine can not cure you
when the education and the educated can solve theorems
but not put two and two together.

we are in trouble and the skies are telling us with its pollution
and the weather is turning a cold shoulder to the changing season in the month of May
and bringing us snow in Missouri
what is natural just isn't normal anymore.
people don't know they have the authority to invite heaven into it all
but they are hungry for hell and something is wrong.

we think we need a plan B for our daughters
what the world needs now is LOVE
we think we need to delete and block the haters
what the world needs now is LOVE
we think we need to threaten other countries with the possibilities of nuclear warfare
what the world needs now is LOVE
we think we need 48 laws of power
what the world needs now is LOVE
we think we need a bad bitch
what the world needs now is LOVE
we think we need some dick
what the world needs now is LOVE
we think we need to come out of our closets
what the world needs now is LOVE
sweet, sweet
LOVE
and willing hearts to produce
and manufacture it
conserve it
preserve it
multiply
and extend it

When Love Finds You (for Lathosa, pronounced *La-tosha*)

sometimes
the first whiff of the aroma is so hearty and filling
that comparing it to fresh bread is best way to describe it
and all the oats and yeast that we've sown starts to rise
we're not slow
so we learn to knead slow
and cast our loaves onto the sea for the fish to eat
and many days after our portions float back,
swollen to feed hundreds, thousands, multitudes a plenty

sometimes
the first encounter to the heat
and culinary technique of our lovers
can turn us from solid to silk
melt our skin into butter
absorb us up into the fabric of the carpet
stain our memories beyond a way to scrub it clean
out of the weft of our thought patterns

love is that way

and sometimes
more often than less
we associate
the meanings
purpose
dimensions
existence
destiny
of a thing, this love thing
with the characteristics of the object that embodies it

as if the color red is solely assigned to an apple
as if the color blue is held hostage at gunpoint by the sky
and shackled with rusty chains to the sea
as if the sight of a smile needs kindness of heart as a pre-qualification to lease
one on a persons facial features
as if its mandatory for the stripes of a zebra to be black and white

it isn't until we take up our cross;

it isn't until we fetch our baskets and saunter to the orchard-
and pick our fruit
that we discover the indecisiveness of a brae burn,
the army fatigue of the honey crisp,
the matured defiance of a granny smith,
the honey blood genetics in a gala,
the humility in the macintosh
or the matte finish of a golden delicious
cause they're all apples anyhow

and if you peer into the great beyond
and offer your heart to the sky,
in the right sunlight
at a new altitude,
with another glance
from a new position on this big wide world
the sky turns a tangy, grapefruit pink
and it will offer you a taste of paradise

the sea has been known to stand high with its chest proud,
tide low and exchange blows within itself
like a mad woman;
or rest peaceful like an elderly woman
hands crossed rocking forward, back
in its currents like a wooden rocker.

devils master beautiful charms
and make snakes dance;
and what is a smile?
just another device for them to use to disarm your defenses

and mother Africa gave birth to Zebras
that appear to have ghost riding on their backs,
finger combing their hair
from mane to tail.

needless to say,
love is a spirit
and when necessary will morph into a new frame,
shift and camouflage its color gradients,
change its extremes from Fahrenheit
and then demand to be read in Celsius

from a different angle it will influence
the depiction of genetics and defy the rules

but of all the wonder love should cause us to possess,
the wonder and the thanksgiving
regardless of the object that it affects or effects

with love you never know which is appropriate terminology to apply
Both terms are subject to apply

should be in the awareness that LOVE found YOU.

not that you were ever without
the GOD/LOVE that is within. so,
red or green,
bite the fruit sent to nourish you
gray for a storm, or summer when it came, dance in the rain
lay lazy in its yellow and expose your face to the sky
admire the sun and be pulled in
admire the Son and be pulled in
guard all that you treasure and that you feel important from the deception of
the thieves that come to steal your heart and identity
and if you never get to visit Africa, know that Albino Zebra exist

sometimes
the impossibilities
and the unimaginable happens
love is a spirit
and we are not equipped, without facing our death,
to lean unto our own understanding and confine it in our own familiarity

within you
out side of you
from you... to you
love & be loved.
love & be love.
love & be, *love.*

Love Thrive In me

freely
flow through me
freely
come to me
freely
thrive within me
spirit of love

teach me life through your compassion
cradle me in your gentle hands
lead me with your light
i am an expression of You
so i am good ground
and love is the seed
there is more than enough for love to be
nourished within me
invited into every action of me
i know you will not come down from heaven
to change what you've equipped my hands
to mend to bind to loose
on Earth
but you'll move
both Heaven and Earth
to prove that you have my best interest at heart
so use your vessels
every spore of the human make up
their entire being
and every circumstances that surround me
inspire them with all you are
to show your dedication towards me
i've always requested that some man do it instead
and i know you sent your son too
but now i am asking of you
to not only love me generally
but tenderly, personally, especially
be in love with me and *allow me the honor to fall in love with you*
help me uphold the conditions of our relationship
there is so much i don't know
so much cleaning up i have to do

i want to know where you are at all times
these eyes to peer wide open and see you in all things
revere you in everyway
and listen to you sing through me
stay with me, never leave me lonely
like a moth to a flame;
gravity over all objects that cannot defy it
like hydrogen to oxygen compounds
that create a life sustaining substance
create new life within me
attract, infuse, draw into me
life filled love

freely
flow through me
freely
come to me
freely
thrive in me
spirit of love

⁝ Gratitude ⁝

[Attitude of Gratitude]

First and foremost, I would like to thank the Sincere, Truthful and Understanding spirit of the living God, Jehovah, Abba, my father for His kindness, compassion, selflessness, and for the opportunity to be a vessel of this gift and of love. Thank you for your son, thank you for His example of perfection and intercession on Earth; thank you for the holy spirit that guides me daily. Though I am imperfect, I want to thank you for allowing me a life to be fruitful in. I appreciate your mercy, your protection and your revelation. Thank you for allowing your spirit of love and creativity to flow through me in any capacity and towards me. Thank you for every door you open, and for every detrimental thing that you have kept me from and removed from my life. Thank you for redirecting the devourer over everything my hand touches. Thank you for blessing me indeed, enlarging my territory, keeping your hand with me, keeping me mindful of your presence, and keeping me from evil, and keeping me from causing harm to others. Thank you for harvesting my seeds of faith. Thank you for wisdom, and understanding. I love you. Thank you for letting me grow in love with you daily. Thank you for being who you are and for all you will do in the future. Thank you, thank you, thank you for being GOOD.

[To My Mother]

Where do I begin? 'I love you' was never easy for you to say but you proved it the best way you knew how. If it were not for you I would not know strength. Being raised by you and under your care I have learned humility and to be thankful for all that God has blessed me with. I have also learned the fear of God through your mighty hand. *laughing* I don't know many people that could have endured what you did alone, even before the six children that you had to raise alone, and manage to keep their sanity. You are a trailblazer. I don't know any profession you haven't had *laughing* and I don't know if there is anything that you couldn't do. I see the way you fight for what you believe in, even when others don't seem to believe in you and you do so with confidence and courage. Its almost like you do it no matter what, just to prove you can, and then you are on to your next adventure. I love that about you. It took me some maturing to appreciate that in you, but I love that in you. Thank you for all things that you have taught me and my brother and sisters and all the things you didn't know how to teach us. Thank you , to date, for becoming a better woman, a better person, a better you. I know you have so many more great things to do in this life and I believe in you like you believe in me. Thank you again for telling me to get off the tree and just fly. I think my wings are big enough now. *smile*

A special thank you to all my family and friends that have given me REAL love, support and strength along the way and the best way that you knew how I love you beyond words can say.

[My Sisters, Aunts, Cousins, Nieces & Close Girlfriends]

Cathiaun (I love *your loyalty &service*), Patrice (*I love your strength of conviction*), Dawn *(I love your sense of self awareness and presence*), Dawnette (*your joy lights up a room, I wish more people had that gift*), Brittany (*how dedicated you are in love, welcome to the family*), Malika (*I love you strong cuzzo, thank you for being there always*), Audrey(*my fitness guru*), Shellon (*thank you for being who you are and knowing who you are),* Triska (*I love our talks and your wisdom is absolutely beautiful*) , Rayana (*you are my sarcasm in human form. I love it*! *You're a wonderful woman and mother hose grown so much*), Natasha(*I appreciate and* admire *your peace and compassion*), Regina (the quiet storm, *20 + years & counting sis , I love you, better or worse*), Monique (*no words to explain what you mean to me, my Angel on Earth! Thank you for all you are and all you've done for me. I love you*), Iyesha (*no one prayers with me like you do, you are so real of a person, thank you for giving it to me like it is and always coming from a place of love*), Courtney *(you are going to be an amazing woman one day, I can just feel it. You've taught me so much more than you know. Stay beautiful*) Meshawn (the *mover & shaker you hold it together so well, and I love that in you*), Whitney(my *baby si, the first person to call and scream with me. I love your sincerity, you are the best!*), Jazmine (you are *so driven, your strength is incredible to me*), Faye *(your humor and your discipline has inspired me so much, thank you*), Candice (*proof that loyalty and patience and transformation exist in people, I love you*), Danat (*you ain't going nowhere, ever! Thank you for being there when I didn't know where I was or who I was becoming*), Brittney(*my brat, I love & miss you like crazy*), Brandi (*your FAITH! If I could have a portion of your courage I would be unstoppable!*), Vanessa M (*super strong woman you are! You loved me always. Thank you for being confident. It inspires me*) Khia aka Finesse (*so proud of you for always being determined to win*), Sherifatu (*nothing like your resiliency*), Ashley Anne (*you are actually the friend I've had the longest...wow...and you have been incredible ever since I've known you thank you for being unchanging and remarkable*), Stella (*thank you for your kindness, sincerity, generosity and advice*) Taylor-Wang (*thank you for being beautiful in more ways than one*), Rhodesia (*them dimples! & your loyalty*), Sasha (*You are just all together fly! & tell it like it is*), Princess (*you're on your way, keep pushing love!*), SueEllen (*you wrote a short story back when I was in the fifth grade and it inspired me to write. I never told you but Thank you for that along with your sense of humor, your drive, your animated personality*) , Tamika Y, Arielle, Destiny, Raven, Elaine (*that voice! I love it! No one goes toe to toe with me on the insults like you. Glad to have gotten close to you cuz*) , Sun-Cirae, DaNiyah (*ILY),* Imani *(my mini me ... one day I will tell you how much you've changed my world.),* Ebony (*Auntie loves you, I will hold your heavy butt forever!*), Linnae (*that voice, that gift is what is don't be afraid*), Brooklynne (*my diva*), Niyah (*my god daughter, love you babygirl*), Phyllicia & Malina (I *love you and miss you much*), Isabella (*that baby got those pretty dimples*), June (*thank you for your sense and focus, to identify with*), Bridgette *(fashionista and the coolest aunt EVER!),* Paulette T(*love & miss you much auntie, thank you for the Toni Morrison book when I was little and for Sula*), Kim (*love & miss you and that good food you make*), Paulette M (*thank you for raising my bestfriend, she is a gift to me and so are you*) , Mary L *(Thank you for adopting me and looking out for me as much as you do. You are the best!),* Michelle, Ana (*a prayer warrior*), Marilyn A (*no one has ever cracked crab legs for me. Ha ha I admire how loving you are, thank you for welcoming me with open arms and genuine love*), Anika (*you are incredible*), Shai (*you're still my bff, I don't care what malika say! Ha ha*)

[My Brothers, Uncles, Cousins, Nephews & Close Guy Friends]

Oswald B (*RIP daddy*), Michael W (*thank you for life, and my brothers and sisters*), Derrick(*my 100%, always*), Eddie (*my heart, thank you for the love in your heart towards me and receiving mine. "A million years and a day."I love you even when it hurts to*), Quillon, Rawle, Michael Jr, Errol (*thank you for introducing me to HipHop and the love of music*), EJ (*so handsome, love you cuzo*), Collis (*you are so gifted and humble and thank you for just being you, you're so cool*), Terrence *(I don't have enough room to thank you for all the inspiration you give me; you are the only other person in this world that is just like me. Glad to see you soaring!*), Stuart *(I knew our "beef" as kids was always misguided love. Ha ha no one gets under my skin like you, that only means you have easier access to my heart, and you will always be there in it cousin. I love your smart mouth!)*, Lil Rennie, Andrew (*its me and you and our weirdness against the world, they'll catch up to us one day ;)*), Drew L (*my play play brother, thank you is an understatement for all the talks and advice. So happy for your new found love. You deserve it!)*Mark (*I love you brother in law*), Troy (*I love you too Wesley Snipes, ha ha*), Lennie (*you're like the OTHER annoying big brother I never had. You are Ren and Troy is Stempy. Lol, love you bro in law*), Robert *(Love you Robert, praying for you always, God has a wonderful plan for your life*), David H (*scratch! You are the best, and you know it ☺keep loving my sis the way you do*), Joshua (*now, I can buy you all the corn you desire *laughing**), Alexi (*fly kidd, you are just dope for no reason*), Rasheid (*you play it low key nephew but I know you are a problem on the low, can't wait to see you blossom*), Issac (*my baby, I love you*) , Javonni (*you're too little to know me but I can't wait to spoil you rotten*), Vincent (*miss you uncle! Even if you laughed at my critter cake*), Clyde (*thank you for being strong and spiritually inclined to support me. I love you so much*), Clive (*I will always be the original mun-chichi, love you uncle!)*, Rennie, Donell (*thank you for taking care of me and my sisters and brother*) Kevin P (*we've been through much thank you for being in my life, congrats on your baby girl, let's get back to work now☺)*, Justin B (*you have always believed in me and I am so grateful for you. Thank you for your individuality inspires me*), Jermin P (*my Guyanese brother! I love you for always having my back and best interest at heart. Never change your cool calm collected ways*), Eric B. Sr (*thank you for the talk, you have been an angel in disguise and I am proud of who you have grown to be. You are amazing. Congrats on the beautiful bride*), Camden (big ol baby blue eyes ;) you are going to be so handsome when you grow up)

[Extended Mothers, Educators, Mentors, Coaches]

Ms. Theresa, Ms. Pam *(you are so sweet on me! Thank you)*, Lenora (*thank you for teaching me "I am enough" and teaching me to accept me for who and what I am. You possess womanhood, and it inspires me tremendously.*), Monifa (*where do I begin? You helped to find my true voice when I was feeling my way through the dark. I never thought I would meet anyone that validated the way I thought and approached music the way you, from the bottom of my heart, thank you so much. I love being your student*), Desilya (*thank you for confidence!)*, Hunter & Ann

Credle (*thank you for believing in me always, that is truly an understatement. You are the best and I am glad we've crosses paths. Thank you for teaching me honesty! I think I am tackling that discipline part now. Ha ha*), Erin P (*you have inspired me to write in such a way I wouldn't have dared to reveal before. It'll only be better from here. I think sharing it was the principle thing in this case. Thank you for all your selflessness. Hope I can repay that somehow and soon!),* J Stone (*thank you for the talks and encouragement*), V. Williams (*thank you for the encouragement. I loved your book "On the Verge of Greatness"! Thank you for letting me proof read it*); thank you to every Pastor that saw in me what I could not see and encouraged me to take a leap of faith. Due to some of the content in this book, I will not list your names out of respect and without consent. Just know you are appreciated GREATLY.

[Extended Friends & Colleagues]

Kat R, Judith, LaShawna, Lathosa, Deborah, Pudgy, Ian, Ant, Nancy Lee, Paula King, Carolyn R, Ms. Gerald, Crystal L, Chaz B, Taronda, Malcolm F, Allison F, Angie & Brad B, Robert W, Bessie E, Greg W, Shirley T, Lessie R, Chiccola B, Christine J, Corey, Jeff F, Deshawn, Demarcus W, Denita S, Dwayne M, Sedrick M, Eric B Sr., Eric B Jr, John Williams, Alicia T, Evin G, Kevin M, Focus Photography, Mel "Punisher", Portia W, Gloria, Hutch, India Mejia, Dawn S, Willie Perdomo, Nikki Nicole, Ava Chin *(thank your acknowledging me*)

Darryl C, Michael C, Chris P, Cedeno, Donell, Supa, Ace, Jay & Tarnisha J, Shaniqua, Jeremiah, Johnny B, Jose R, Juan S, Lynette S, Justin A, Keisha W, Ken Shields, Kevin Shine, Lamont R, Mr. & Mrs. Gutierrez, Emmanuel & Greg, Maggie, Marcus F, Cathy M, Lita, Millie Vaughn, Ms Dorothy, Gerald L, Omega Red, S. Gold, S. Towns, Steve W, Stormie F, Tara H, T Covington, Tia Nate,

Tiffany Souletic & hubby Akeem, Tonya M, Victor D, Virginia B, Wendy, Ximena, Jason, Sharon B, Latonya, Doug M, Nicole, Donell A, Crystal M, Bubacarr D, Deone Mitchell, Chrstina N, Sean R, Reena J, Dell F, Tiffany Denae, Gabrielle B, Tenia C, Rolando J, Jammie S, Chris P, Maya, Larisha, Nasira, Pamela W, Bernadette J, Brad B, Caesar B, Kelly H, Jeanette E, Andria H, Camellia, Latissa, Ashleigh T, Ashley F, Tameeka, Renaldo, Niko, Verne, Chelsea, Matt G, Shawn W,

Adon Cooper, Sean Anthony

If I have failed to include your name, please count it to my head and not my heart. I didn't realize that God blessed me with an abundance of people to show and bring love into my life, as a result, its hard to remember in detail every instance in which all the amazing people I know have changed and influenced my life. But you ALL have! I am so thankful for you all and I appreciate all the love you have shown me in any capacity.

[My Readers]

THANK YOU!!!!!

Love *always*, *Danielle*

ABOUT THE AUTHOR

Danielle BlaiQ is a published Author, aspiring Hip Hop-Soul Music Artist, Songwriter and dabbles in most things that pertain to the performing arts. Born in Brooklyn, New York and raised outside Raleigh, North Carolina; she is the 5th girl of six children. She is first generation born in the United States, her family bloodline with ties to South America.

Danielle has been and avid writer and has been writing poetry, and short stories since the age of 7 years old. Aside from writing, drawing, performing arts and music, she takes interest in traveling, learning new cultures, biblical studies, world religions, holistic living, women's health, fitness, relationships, print modeling, and meeting new people from different walks of life.

Danielle currently resides in the south eastern part of the United States working full time with Autistic men and women. She is welcoming new opportunities to share her works and grow personally and artistically.

Visit Danielle's site:

www.DanielleBlaiQ.com

via twitter: *@blaiQangel*

www.ingramcontent.com/pod-product-compliance
Lightning Source LLC
LaVergne TN
LVHW041221080426
835508LV00011B/1033
* 9 7 8 0 6 1 5 8 1 4 5 2 0 *